W9-BZC-169

EVERYDAY EASY

EVERYDAY EASY
Lorraine Pascale

Photographs by Myles New

ecco

An Imprint of HarperCollinsPublishers

HarperCollins books may be purchased for educational, business, or sales promotional use. For information please e-mail the Special Markets Department at SPsales@harpercollins.com.

First published under the title *Fast, Fresh and Easy Food* in Great Britain in 2012 by HarperCollins Publishers UK, 77-85 Fulham Palace Road, Hammersmith, London W68JB.

FIRST U.S. EDITION

Food styling: Katie Giovanni and Julia Azzarello
Prop styling: Lisa Harrison

Library of Congress Cataloging-in-Publication Data has been applied for.

ISBN 978-0-06-230579-4

15 16 17 18 19   IN/QGT   10 9 8 7 6 5 4 3 2 1

Contents

Introduction

Staring at the blank page with my deadline looming, no words seemed to be coming. A relaxed, unpressurized atmosphere is usually when a flurry of inspiration hits, but it wasn't until I was on a plane ride home from sunny, siliconed Los Angeles with a glass of Californian Chardonnay on my tiny table that the words began to flow.

I thought back to my first book, *Baking Made Easy*, a self-explanatory title packed with recipes that, in my own words, covered "anything cooked in the oven." The broad definition allowed me artistic license to develop meals and dishes both sweet and savory. Exotic tarts and traditional cakes featured alongside nighttime nibbles and Parisian patisserie. With my next book, *Home Cooking Made Easy*, came food with a more homey note: comforting casseroles and lasagnes, beauteous breads and simple desserts.

It felt, for the meantime anyway, that I'd had a significant part of my cooking repertoire covered and that this time I wanted to try something a little bit different, something that would hopefully prove even more useful for the (sadly) ever-decreasing time in which we have to prepare and cook food. I don't know how often I have come home from a day whizzing around like the Energizer Bunny on the rampage to a family awaiting some culinary delight. I also don't know how many times I have hung my head in shame and uttered the words, "Oh. Yes. Dinner," and then made the short trip to the local supermarket to try to buy from the near-empty shelves and then cobble something together for dinner.

I am not at all embarrassed to say that on many occasions I have returned home to the waiting party laden with food that just needs a simple peeling back of the plastic and a slight turn of the oven dial, usually to 350°F. These ready-meals serve a purpose and I am thankful that they exist, but I wondered about a book that was jam-packed full of dishes that were quick, simple, nutritious and above all supertasty. I wrote this book for the many, many people out there who, like me and my family, face the same daily dilemma of "What on earth is for dinner?"

Thanks to the brilliant medium of Twitter, countless readers have told me that the important thing for the evening meal is that it is easy and quick to cook, using ingredients that don't require a space shuttle flight to the outer reaches of the solar system to source. The main ingredients people seem to favor are chicken (breasts, not so much the thigh or the leg), lamb chops, pork chops, ground beef or lamb, and fish. So I've included an enormous range of dishes featuring these, along with other tasty fare such as duck and vegetarian grub. I don't know if it is the Brit in me, but with my meal I like to eat some kind of a veg and/or a carb, but not any ordinary side dish—something a bit different that will leave (even with the quickest of meals) a lasting sensory memory on my tongue and in my mind.

Dishes such as the Italian cacciatore get a gentle lift with the help of the mildly spiced harissa, a red chilli paste from North Africa. A simple salmon en croute is transformed by the use of papery phyllo in which to envelop it, and the accompanying potatoes are gently crushed with a pesto made from basil and curly kale. A lamb biryani, cooked in one pot and ready to eat in 25 minutes, is delicately spiced with the very-easy-to-find garam masala, cumin and chilli powder.

My current favorite is Lemoncello Jell-O Shots—lemon wedges scraped clean of their flesh and filled with a citrusy alcoholic (or not, if you so choose) jelly—which is so simple to make and yet so attention-getting when served, and of course superyumbelicious to eat.

The goal of this book was to create something people would revisit time and time again. A cookbook that would be on that kitchen counter several times a week, for busy people who love good food and want to make something quick and easy, with tasty and accessible ingredients, to impress family and friends. And I wanted to provide an entire meal: main dish and side. So often when you know what you want to cook, it is challenging to figure out what to have with it. With this book, I have served up dishes with an accompaniment or two, making mealtimes much easier to plan. I also tried to make it as simple as possible so that everything is served up together, with a time plan for each recipe so you can sail through the instructions and end up with a delicious dish in superfast time. I have put my heart and soul into this book and hope it helps you to serve up fast, fresh and delicious meals every day.

Lorraine

A few handy tips on the recipes

+ All preparation and cooking times are estimates, so check and taste things as they cook.

+ Always wash rice thoroughly before use.

+ I find it best to have all the ingredients and equipment ready before you start cooking, so everything is easy to get when you need it.

+ These recipes have all been tested a minimum of four times, and they have been written so that everything is ready at the same time. So if you follow the method to the letter you will have quick and tasty meals ready in flash.

+ Some recipes have a start-to-finish time so you know roughly how long it will take from the moment you start cooking to when you finish.

+ Other recipes are split between preparation time and cooking/baking time. So the prep time is the hands-on time and the rest of the time while the dish is in the oven is free time!

+ Some recipes are superfast and others have an element to them that is faster than the usual way of prepping or cooking the dish.

+ The equipment list is not exhaustive but a guide to the main pieces of kitchen equipment you will need to prepare the dish. Everyday smaller utensils required are not included in the list.

+ If you have any cooking questions, please do Tweet me @lorrainepascale. I receive lots of Tweets and cannot guarantee to answer every one, but I will do my best!

Canapés + cocktails

Be kind, for everyone you meet is fighting a hard battle.
Plato

I would love to profess that friends drop by
unexpectedly, so I have to rustle something up quickly
for an impromptu feast, but the reality is that never
really happens. What does tend to happen is that,
in true Lorraine Pascale style, I am always rushing
around, slightly disorganized and with the clock ticking
away, having known for weeks that some people
are coming round and always leaving it to the very
last minute to get everything together! These simple
canapés (and of course cocktails) are the perfect
solution to this modern-day madness of rush, rush,
rush. So easy to prepare and supertasty too,
with that ever-important "wow" factor on the plate.

Time from start to finish:
20 minutes
Makes: 24
Equipment: Large baking sheet,
3 small bowls

Crostini bases

1 French baguette
Extra virgin olive oil
1 garlic clove

Tomato, basil & mint

2 large ripe tomatoes
Extra virgin olive oil
Small handful of fresh basil and
mint leaves
Salt and freshly ground pepper
Pinch of sugar (optional)

White bean, prosciutto & arugula

4 oz canned (½ cup) cannellini beans
Extra virgin olive oil
Salt and freshly ground pepper
2 slices of prosciutto
Small handful of wild arugula

Goat cheese, figs & mint with balsamic drizzle

4 oz soft goat cheese
Salt and freshly ground pepper
2 fresh figs
Small handful of small fresh mint leaves
Drizzle of balsamic vinegar
1 squeeze or dab of honey

Quick-cook canapé crostini

These really easy canapés have saved the day, not only when (in the very rare event) people drop by my house unannounced, but also when I fancy a quick snack in the evening. It is great to get creative with these: see what is in your cupboard and fridge, throw some ingredients together and experiment! I have used the oven to crisp up the crostini, but they can be put in the toaster or under the broiler to get the same effect. If you crisp them up first, they won't need as much time to cook.

+ Preheat the oven to 375°F.

+ Trim the ends off the baguette and cut it into 24 diagonal slices, about ¾ inch thick. Place on a large baking sheet, drizzle with oil and bake for 7–8 minutes.

+ In the meantime, prepare the toppings.

+ For the tomato one, roughly chop the tomatoes and place in a small bowl. Drizzle a little oil over, rip up the basil and mint leaves and add them along with salt, pepper and sugar to taste. Toss everything together.

+ Then, for the white bean topping, put the cannellini beans in a small bowl, add a good drizzle of oil, season with salt and pepper and then mash roughly with a fork. Cut the slices of prosciutto in quarters.

+ Finally, for the goat cheese crostini, mash the goat cheese with a fork in a small bowl and season, then cut the figs into eighths.

+ Remove the crostini from the oven. They should be just crisp. Cut the garlic clove in half and rub the cut edge all over their tops.

+ Now, to assemble, simply spoon the tomato mixture onto eight of the crostini. Arrange the arugula on eight more, dollop the crushed beans on top, then lightly scrunch up the prosciutto and arrange on top of each one. Finally, spread the goat cheese over the remaining eight crostini, arrange a couple of pieces of fig on top of each, scatter the mint leaves over and drizzle with a little balsamic and honey.

+ Arrange the crostini on a large serving platter or cake stand and serve.

Time from start to finish:
25 minutes
Serves: 4
Equipment: Baking tray, 2 wide, shallow bowls, small bowl

Vegetable oil (or spray oil)

2 medium eggs

4 oz (½ cup) dried plain breadcrumbs (or polenta)

1 tsp English mustard powder

2 stalks of fresh flat leaf parsley or thyme (optional)

Salt and freshly ground black pepper

4 medium skinless, boneless chicken breasts

Honey mustard dip

½ cup mayonnaise

3 tbsp whole grain mustard

2 squeezes or dabs of honey

Salt and freshly ground black pepper

2 limes

Crispy, crunchy chicken strips with honey mustard dip

Being a tactile person at heart, eating food with my fingers is pure luxury for me. I have a favorite surf-and-turf restaurant I frequent with the family and I regularly order their crispy chicken tenders for a starter. The piquant honey mustard dip has me getting right on in there with a spoon and eating up every last morsel.

+ Preheat the oven to 400°F. Lightly grease a baking tray with oil and set aside. I like to do this quickly with a spray oil.

+ Crack the eggs into a wide, shallow bowl and beat lightly to bring together. Put the breadcrumbs (or polenta) and mustard powder into another wide, shallow bowl. Pick the leaves from the parsley or thyme and then finely chop them before tossing with the breadcrumbs and some salt and pepper.

+ Cut each chicken breast lengthwise into three strips. Dip each piece into the egg, shaking off the excess, and then into the breadcrumbs to coat evenly. Arrange on the baking tray as you go. I tend to get in a sticky mess with this as the egg on my hands becomes coated with breadcrumbs, but the end result is so worth it.

+ Bake in the oven for around 12 minutes, turning each piece of chicken over halfway through.

+ Meanwhile, to make the dip, put the mayonnaise into a small bowl with the whole grain mustard and honey and stir to combine. Season to taste with salt and pepper.

+ Cut the limes into quarters and add the juice of one piece to the dip, squeeze by squeeze, tasting as you go until you are happy. The lime lifts the dip's flavors a little and gives a nice balance. Spoon the dip into a small serving bowl and place in the center of a large plate.

+ Remove the chicken from the oven. When cooked, it should be piping hot in the center and crispy and golden brown on the outside.

+ Arrange the chicken around the dip on a plate and serve with the remaining lime wedges.

Prep time: 25 minutes
Time baking in the oven:
25 minutes
Makes: About 25
Equipment: 2 baking sheets,
small frying pan, medium
saucepan, grater, 2 medium
bowls, disposable piping bag
(optional)

4 tbsp butter

½ cup milk

2 oz pancetta cubes

Oil

1 oz Parmesan cheese

½ cup all-purpose flour

1 tsp chilli powder (optional)

Pinch of salt

2 medium eggs

Pancetta & Parmesan puffs

I know, I have done it again. Pancetta. It's that porky, tasty yumminess that I love so very much. Now these cheesy little numbers are made from choux pastry, which for me is the easiest pastry on the block. A positive word of warning: these are incredibly yummy. A just-cooked bowl of them will disappear in literally minutes.

+ Preheat the oven to 325°F. Line two baking sheets with baking parchment and set aside.

+ Put a small frying pan on a medium heat for the pancetta.

+ Put the butter and milk in a medium saucepan over a low heat and leave the butter to melt.

+ Meanwhile, place the pancetta in the frying pan with a drizzle of oil and cook for about 4 minutes, turning every so often.

+ Once the butter has melted into the milk, turn up the heat and bring to the boil.

+ Meanwhile, finely grate the Parmesan and put it into a medium bowl. Stir in the flour, chilli powder, if you like, and a pinch of salt.

+ As soon as the buttery milk boils, remove the pan from the heat and add the flour mixture to it. Beat it really hard with a wooden spoon until the mixture starts to leave the sides of the pan. Then transfer to a medium bowl, spread it out all around the inside and leave it for a few minutes until cool to the touch.

+ Once the pancetta is crisp and golden, remove from the heat and put on paper towels to drain off excess fat and set aside.

+ Once the flour mix has cooled down a little, add the eggs, one at a time, beating hard after each addition. When the egg first goes in, the mixture will look a little less than pleasant, as if it won't mix in, but keep beating it really hard and it will blend well. Then stir in the pancetta.

+ Now, here you can either spoon blobs of the choux pastry onto the baking sheets or (my favorite method with my piping bag obsession)

>

Pancetta &
Parmesan puffs

(continued)

pipe the blobs using a disposable piping bag cut to give a ½ inch opening. Either way, make them about ¾–1¼ inches in diameter and space them a little bit apart. This makes about 25. Use a finger slightly moistened with water to push down any end bits that may be sticking up (so they don't burn in the oven), then bake for 25 minutes.

+ The puffs should be crisp and golden on top when cooked. These are really best served piping hot while they are still slightly moist when they are cut open.

Time from start to finish:
15 minutes
Serves: 4
Equipment: Colander, blender
or food processor, large frying
pan

Hummus

14-oz can of chickpeas

I garlic clove

4 oz low- or full-fat crème fraîche

1–4 tbsp harissa paste (easy to find at
the supermarket)

Salt and freshly ground black pepper

Drizzle of extra virgin olive oil
(optional)

Halloumi

Sunflower oil

Pepper

⅓ cup all-purpose flour

Two 9-oz blocks of halloumi cheese

1 lime

Small handful of fresh cilantro

Salt and freshly ground black pepper

Crunchy black pepper halloumi dip sticks with harissa hummus

Before I tested this recipe I had not had the privilege of cooking halloumi. I'd eaten it many times, but never felt the urge to give it a go at home. Halloumi is an eccentric-textured-and-tasting cheese which is very salty on the palate. It prefers, unlike its cheesy counterparts, to be pan-fried and grilled as it holds itself together very well once cooked.

+ First, make the hummus. Drain and rinse the chickpeas, peel the garlic and add both to a blender or food processor. Add the crème fraîche and enough harissa paste to taste (depending on how hot you like it). Blitz until smooth, season to taste with salt and pepper and add a drizzle of oil if you think it needs it. Then spoon it into a serving bowl and set aside.

+ Next, prepare the halloumi. Put three big glugs of oil in a large frying pan over a medium heat. Put the flour on a plate, season with a little pepper and set aside. Cut the halloumi into thick sticks. I cut each block into quarters lengthwise and then lay each piece on its side and cut it in half again to give eight big chunky chips. Toss them in the flour so they are well covered, then gently lower them into the hot oil and fry for 4–5 minutes, turning regularly with tongs, until golden brown all over.

+ Remove the halloumi from the pan and drain on paper towels for a minute. Then arrange on a large serving plate and squeeze the lime juice over. Sit the dip bowl on the plate beside the halloumi, pick and scatter the cilantro leaves on top and serve. Halloumi really comes to life with these flavors.

Naughty, naughty nachos

Time from start to finish:
25 minutes
Serves: 6
Equipment: Colander, 2 small
bowls, 9- or 10-inch square
baking dish at least 2 inches
deep

Salsa

7-oz jar red or green jalapeños

8 oz (½ pint) cherry tomatoes

1 red onion (or 1 bunch of green onions)

Small handful of fresh cilantro

Nachos

7 oz Cheddar cheese

14-oz can of kidney beans

7-oz bag of tortilla chips

7 oz (¾ cup + 2 tbsp) sour cream

Guacamole

3 perfectly ripe avocados

A few drops of Tabasco sauce (optional)

Salt and freshly ground black pepper

½ lime

Lots of cheese, chips and cream. Just what I feel I need on those days when I want that extra bit of comfort on a plate. There are a few parts to this recipe, but it is really, really quick and I find myself gravitating to make this on the weekend, as it is a great sharing dish. It is on the side of naughty, but really tasty. Everything in balance is my mantra. I found the jars of jalapeños in the supermarket, but if you can't get them, just use two regular green or red chillies, seeded and finely sliced.

+ Preheat the oven to 400°F.

+ First, prepare the salsa. Drain the jalapeños, quarter the cherry tomatoes and toss both into a small bowl. Peel and finely chop the red onion (or finely slice the green onions, if using), reserve a small handful and add the remainder to the bowl. Rip the leaves from the cilantro stalks, roughly chop them, then toss everything together and season to taste.

+ Finely grate the cheese and drain and rinse the beans.

+ Now to assemble the nachos. Scatter a third of the tortilla chips in the bottom of the baking dish and scatter over a third of the cheese and then all of the beans. Then follow with a third more tortillas, a third more cheese and some of the salsa. Finish with the remaining tortillas and cheese. This is actually a total free-form dish; my only thing is I love cheese on the top.

+ Now pop it into the oven to bake for 10 minutes while you make the guacamole.

+ Halve the avocados, discard the pits and use a spoon to scoop the flesh out into a small bowl. Lightly mash with a fork and then mix the reserved chopped onion with a few drops of Tabasco, if you like. Season to taste with salt and pepper and squeeze in the lime juice.

+ Spoon the sour cream, remaining salsa and guacamole into small serving bowls. Remove the now-cooked nachos from the oven. The cheese should be bubbling and the tortillas just catching color. Serve in the center of the table with the accompaniments for everyone to dig in and help themselves.

Skinny dipping

Three tasty, no-cook skinny dip numbers; great to eat with crispy potato skins, tortilla chips or crudités such as carrots, radishes and celery. You can make them all or just one or two. They can all be made ahead of time for stress-free snacking!

Tuna & crème fraîche dip with black pepper
Makes: About 1 cup

6- or 7-oz can of tuna in spring water
⅓ cup low- or full-fat crème fraîche
A few fresh chives
Salt and freshly ground black pepper
¼ lime (or lemon)
Teeny dab of honey (optional)

Hummus with cumin & paprika
Makes: About 1½ cups

14-oz can of chickpeas
½ cup low- or full-fat crème fraîche
2 tsp cumin powder
Extra virgin olive oil
1 garlic clove
Salt and freshly ground black pepper
¼ lime (or lemon)
A good pinch of paprika
A few fresh cilantro or flat leaf parsley leaves

Avocado, chilli & chive dip
Makes: About 1¼ cups

2 ripe avocados
1 small red chilli
A few fresh chives
Salt and freshly ground black pepper
1 lime (or lemon)

Tuna & crème fraîche dip with black pepper
+ Drain the tuna well, squeezing out as much of the water as possible. Place in a medium bowl, add the crème fraîche and then snip in the chives using scissors. Mix together well and season to taste with salt, pepper and a good squeeze of lime (or lemon) juice. Add a little honey to sweeten, if desired. Spoon into a serving bowl to serve.

Hummus with cumin & paprika
+ Drain the chickpeas, rinse well and then put them into a blender (I find an immersion blender brilliant). Add the crème fraîche, cumin and a drizzle of oil, then peel and add the garlic clove. Season well with salt and pepper and blitz until fairly smooth. Check the seasoning, adjusting if necessary, add a squeeze of lime (or lemon) juice and then blitz again briefly. Spoon into a serving bowl, sprinkle the paprika on top, rip over some cilantro or parsley leaves and serve.

Avocado, chilli & chive dip
+ Cut the avocados in half, discard the pits and then scoop out the flesh into a medium bowl. Seed and finely slice the chilli and add. Then, using scissors, snip in the chives. Mash everything up until fairly smooth, season to taste with a good amount of salt and pepper and squeeze in the lime (or lemon) juice. Spoon into a serving bowl to serve.

Lemoncello Jell-O shots

Prep time: 15 minutes
Setting time: 30 minutes in the
freezer (or 1 hour in the fridge)
Makes: 20–28 (depending on the
size of lemons used)
Equipment: Kettle, small wide
bowl, large tray or 12-cup muffin
pan, heatproof measuring cup

Seven 2½ x 4½-inch or eight
3 x 4-inch leaves of gelatin

7 medium or 5 big lemons

4-oz package of lemon gelatin

1¾ cups hot water

Couple of small drops of lemon
essence (optional)

1 tbsp sugar

Remove these sassy sunshine slices from the freezer or fridge an hour or so before you want to use them so they soften slightly before eating. Of course, these can be made for the kiddies, but for adults I like to add a generous ½ cup of lovely, luscious limoncello (see page 35) to 1¾ cups of water. No need to heat it; just dissolve the jelly in boiling water, add the gelatin leaves, then finish with the limoncello and sugar.

+ Put the kettle on to boil. Then put the gelatin leaves into a small wide bowl, cover them with cold water and set aside to soften.

+ Cut the lemons in half lengthwise and, using a spoon, scoop out the juicy flesh. It takes a bit of wiggling and getting squirted by the juice, but you will get there! The trick is not to break through the skin. (You don't need the flesh here, but afterward I like to squeeze the juice out and freeze it in an ice-cube tray for handy lemon juice needs at other times.)

+ Set each lemon shell half, cut side up, on a large tray, or put each one in the cup of a 12-cup muffin pan. If you have 14 shells, then nestle the remaining two on top in between the others and they should sit still.

+ Next, break up the lemon gelatin a bit and put it into a heatproof measuring cup, then pour over enough hot water to reach 1¾ cups.

+ Pick up the gelatin leaves—they will feel all soft. Gently squeeze out as much liquid as you can from them, discard the bowl of water and then put the soft gelatin leaves into the gelatin and hot water. Stir constantly until they dissolve. Then stir in the lemon essence, if using (sometimes the lemon gelatin just is not lemony enough), and sugar until dissolved.

+ Use the gelatin to fill each lemon shell right up to the very top so it is almost overflowing. Let the shells cool down for about 5 minutes and then put them in the freezer for 30 minutes to firm up (but not much longer or they will freeze!). They will set in the fridge also, but allow double the time.

+ Once they are firm, remove them from the freezer (or fridge). Then, using a sharp, nonserrated knife, cut them in half, straight down, lengthwise, and there you have it!

Prep time: 25 minutes
Setting time: 25 minutes in the freezer, plus 15 minutes if using passion fruit seeds
Makes: 56–64 (depending on the size of limes used)
Equipment: Kettle, small wide bowl, large tray or 2–3 12-cup muffin pans, heatproof measuring cup

Seven 2½ x 4½-inch or eight 3 x 4-inch leaves of gelatin

16 small or 14 medium limes

4-oz package of strawberry gelatin

1¾ cups hot water

1 tbsp sugar (optional)

1 large or 2 small passion fruit (optional)

Watermelon Jell-O shots

If you were a sporty type at school, you may remember those little orange slices that were given out at half time during matches. A momentary respite from jumping and leaping in the air on a cold windy netball court in the depths of winter seems to be a vivid memory from my early teenage years. Naturally, giving you a recipe for orange slices may have proven uninspiring so, with a bit of cooking magic, I would like to introduce you to my watermelon Jell-O shots. . . . A happy walk down memory lane with a very modern twist. For an alcoholic version, replace ½ cup of the water with some vodka.

+ Put the kettle on to boil. Then put the gelatin leaves into a small wide bowl, cover them with cold water and set aside to soften.

+ Cut the limes in half lengthwise, rather than around their middles, and, using a spoon, scoop out the juicy flesh. It takes a bit of wiggling and getting squirted by the juice, but you will get there! The trick is not to break through the lime skin. (You don't need the flesh for this recipe, but afterward I like to squeeze the juice out and freeze it in an ice-cube tray for handy lime juice needs at other times.)

+ Set each half, cut side up, on a large tray, or put each one in the cup of a 12-cup muffin pan. They fit perfectly and don't move around too much that way. You will need two or three 12-cup muffin pans, but if you don't have enough, you can nestle the excess lime shells on top in between the others and they should sit still.

+ Next, break up the strawberry gelatin a bit and put it into a heatproof measuring cup, then pour over enough hot water to reach 1¾ cups.

+ Pick up the gelatin leaves—they will feel all soft. Gently squeeze out as much liquid as you can from them, discard the bowl of water and then put the soft gelatin leaves into the gelatin and hot water. Leave to stand for a few minutes until everything begins to melt, then stir a little until everything is completely dissolved. Next, stir in the sugar, if using, until dissolved also.

>

Watermelon Jell-O shots

(continued)

+ Use the gelatin to fill each lime shell right up to the very top so it is almost overflowing. Let the shells cool down for about 5 minutes and then put them in the freezer for about 25 minutes to firm up (but not much longer or they will freeze!). They will set in the fridge also, but allow double the time.

+ Meanwhile, prepare the passion fruit by cutting it (or them) in half and scooping out the seeds onto paper towels. Dab the seeds dry with the towels and set them aside.

+ Halfway through the setting time (once the gelatins are just beginning to firm up), remove them and carefully arrange the passion fruit seeds on top. Arrange about six seeds on each one, keeping them away from the middle as you will be cutting them in half later, and lightly press each one down a little so it will set into the gelatin. Then return to the freezer until completely firm.

+ Once they are firm, remove them from the freezer. Then, using a sharp, nonserrated knife, cut them in half, straight down (again, lengthwise), and there you have it!

Strawberry & mint mojitos

Time from start to finish:
15 minutes
Makes: **4**
Equipment: **Four 11-oz glasses,
rolling pin, straws or cocktail
stirrers**

3 limes

8 tbsp demerara sugar

12 strawberries

1¾ cups crushed ice

Small handful of fresh mint

1 cup white rum

1 cup soda water or lemonade
(or even Pimm's)

Ahh, mojitos. My Achilles heel, for sure. Whether they be alcoholic or virgin, I love these sugary South American drinks. Strawberries can be substituted with other fruit, such as blackberries or raspberries, and the rum replaced with extra soda water or lemonade for a nonalcoholic version.

+ Cut the limes into quarters lengthwise and put three pieces in the bottom of each of four 11-oz serving glasses. Make sure the glasses are wide enough to fit the end of a rolling pin in. (You'll see why.)

+ Add 2 tablespoons of the sugar to each one. Then, using the end of a rolling pin, squash everything together to squeeze the lime juice out and mix with the sugar.

+ Hull the strawberries (cut out the green bit with the point of a sharp knife) and add three to each glass. Then very gently crush them a bit too.

+ Fill the glasses almost to the top with the crushed ice. Pick and reserve four nice mint sprigs from the bunch and then rip the leaves off the remaining stalks and scatter them onto the ice. Divide the rum evenly among the glasses and then top with the soda water or lemonade.

+ Mix everything together with a spoon, then add a sprig of mint to each glass and serve at once with a straw or cocktail stirrer popped in.

Prep time: 10 minutes
Infusing time: From 1 day to
3 months
Makes: 1 quart
Equipment: Medium saucepan,
zester, 1-quart glass bottle with
a stopper or a Ball jar (sterilized—
see headnote), fine sieve

1⅓ cups granulated sugar

¾ cup cold water

8 lemons

2½ cups vodka

Lovely limoncello

To prepare the containers for this luscious lemon drink, sterilize a 1-quart glass bottle with a stopper or a Ball jar in the dishwasher on the hottest wash, or carefully put it in just-boiled water (off the heat) for a couple of minutes and dry with a clean tea towel.

+ Put the sugar in a medium saucepan over a low to medium heat with the water. Cook for a few minutes, giving it a stir from time to time, until the sugar has melted. Then turn up the heat, bring to the boil and leave to bubble away for 2 minutes.

+ Meanwhile, give the lemons a wash in hot soapy water to get rid of the shiny, waxy coating and then rinse and dry them well. Finely grate the zest, avoiding the white pith, and set aside.

+ Remove the syrup from the heat, carefully add the vodka and stir in the lemon zest.

+ Pour into the sterilized bottle or jar and leave to infuse for at least 1 day, but up to 3 months. The flavor will develop further the longer you leave it.

+ Once ready, strain the liquid through a fine sieve to remove the zest. Serve freezer cold.

Starters, snacks + soups

Not to try is a greater hazard than to fail.
Francis Bacon

My first experience with soup was the rich, red tomato variety, poured straight from a can, but as I learned more about food, I began to see that there was so much more to soup than that. My idea of a soup is something jam-packed full of taste and texture, with layers and layers of flavor, which can be achieved in a reasonable time span for maximum impact. I love to make large batches of soup and pour some into a thermos for part of my lunch. Of course, other light bites such as Aussie Sweet Corn Breakfast Fritters (page 45) are a must when a small meal is desired or as a precursor to a larger one. I wasn't sure where on earth to put my Pizza Expressed Three Ways (page 41), and so placed it in this chapter for a pleasing light bite.

Time from start to finish:
20 minutes (+ ideally 6 hours in
the fridge)
Serves: 4
Equipment: Medium frying pan,
food processor, 4 6-oz ramekins

Oil

2 tbsp butter

2 shallots

3 garlic cloves

1 lb cremini or black poplar
mushrooms

4 tbsp port (optional)

Salt and freshly ground black pepper

2 sprigs of fresh tarragon

4 oz cooked chestnuts (available
vac packed or canned from the
supermarket)

11 oz cream cheese

Your favorite bread, crackers or
breadsticks, to serve

Vegetarian mushroom & port "faux gras" with tarragon & chestnuts

Great for presents, these ramekins will keep in the fridge for up to 4 days. I have been known to give these little bad boys away as part of a basket at Christmas and they are good to have on hand, year round, as a really tasty snack.

+ Put a drizzle of oil and the butter in a medium frying pan over a low heat.

+ Peel and finely chop the shallots and garlic and add to the pan. Cook for 3 minutes, stirring now and again, until soft and slightly golden.

+ Finely slice the mushrooms. Add them to the pan along with the port, if using, and season with salt and pepper. Turn up the heat to medium and cook for 8 minutes, or until the mushrooms have softened and all their liquid has evaporated.

+ Meanwhile, pick the leaves from one sprig of tarragon, divide the other sprig into four smaller pieces and then roughly chop the chestnuts.

+ Transfer the cooked mushroom mixture to a food processor with the chestnuts, individual leaves of tarragon and the cream cheese. Blitz for a few minutes until really smooth, scraping down the sides of the bowl once or twice. Have a taste of it and adjust the seasoning if necessary.

+ Divide among the ramekins, smooth their tops and place a tarragon sprig on top of each to decorate. Arrange them on a small tray or plate, cover with plastic wrap and refrigerate for at least 6 hours or overnight. You can also serve these straightaway, but their texture will be much softer and flavor not so intense. Serve with your favorite bread, crackers or breadsticks.

Time from start to finish:
40 minutes (for all three pizza toppings)
or
Dough: 15 minutes prep
Toppings: 5 minutes per pizza
Time baking in the oven:
8–10 minutes
Makes: 3 thin 4 x 6-inch pizza crusts
Equipment: Large bowl, freestanding electric mixer fitted with the dough hook (optional), rolling pin, 3 baking sheets, clean tea towel (or plastic wrap), scissors, blender, peeler

Pizza dough

2 cups plus 2 tbsp bread flour, plus a little extra for dusting

One ¼-oz package of fast-acting dried yeast

1½ tsp salt

3 tbsp extra virgin olive oil, plus extra for oiling

¾ cup warm tap water (not too hot)

Pizza expressed three ways

You can either make the dough from scratch for this pizza, which takes no time at all, or for an even speedier method, buy soft tortillas and use these as a base for the pizza instead of making your own crust.

+ Preheat the oven to 475°F.

+ Put the flour, yeast and salt into a large bowl and stir to combine. Make a well in the center and add the oil and the water. Then mix it all together with a wooden spoon to form a soft, slightly sticky ball.

+ At this stage I like to get my hands into the bowl and squoosh everything together. Then throw a little flour on the work surface and knead the dough for 8 minutes by hand (or 4 minutes in a freestanding electric mixer fitted with a dough hook).

+ Divide the dough into three equal(ish) pieces and then use a rolling pin to roll each one out into roughly a 4 x 6-inch rectangle. It will be really nice and thin. Put the rectangles on an oiled baking sheet and cover with a clean tea towel or some oiled plastic wrap so they do not dry out while you prepare the toppings. There are three delicious toppings on the next page—each recipe provides enough to top one pizza crust. You can make one pizza using the topping you like or make three to try each of them!

>

Harissa, chilli & sausage pizza with fennel seed & arugula

2 green onions
1 red chilli (optional)
2 fat sausages
2 tbsp harissa paste (found in most supermarkets)
2 tsp fennel seed
Salt and freshly ground black pepper
A handful of wild arugula
Drizzle of extra virgin olive oil

Goat cheese & sweet pepper pizza with chorizo

2 oz (¼ cup) tomato purée or paste
2 oz mild or hot Peppadew peppers (jars are available in most supermarkets)
3 sprigs of fresh thyme
1 garlic clove
3 oz goat cheese
10 chorizo slices
Salt and freshly ground black pepper
Small handful of fresh basil leaves
Drizzle of extra virgin olive oil

Feta, hummus & zucchini pizza with balsamic drizzle & mint

4 oz (½ cup) hummus
4 oz feta cheese
½ small zucchini
6 cherry tomatoes
Salt and freshly ground black pepper
Drizzle of balsamic glaze (found in the supermarket)
Extra virgin olive oil
Small handful of fresh mint leaves

Harissa, chilli & sausage pizza with fennel seed & arugula

+ Trim and finely slice the onions (both the green and the white bits), then halve, seed and finely slice the red chilli, if using, and set aside.

+ Snip the skin off the sausages and then peel it off or squeeze the sausage meat out. Break the sausage meat into small pieces.

+ Spread the harissa paste all over the pizza crust. I like to leave a ¼-inch border, for aesthetic purposes only! Scatter over the onions, chilli, sausage meat and fennel seed and season with a little salt and pepper.

Goat cheese & sweet pepper pizza with chorizo

+ Put the tomato purée and Peppadew peppers in a blender. Run your fingers down the length of the thyme sprigs to release their leaves, peel the garlic and add both to the blender. Blitz until smooth and then spread over the pizza crust, leaving a ¼-inch border.

+ Break the goat cheese into small pieces and scatter over the pizza along with the chorizo slices. Season with a little salt and pepper.

Feta, hummus & zucchini pizza with balsamic drizzle & mint

+ Spread the hummus over the pizza crust and crumble the feta on top. Use a vegetable peeler to slice the zucchini into long, thin strips. Keep going until all is used up and arrange these also. Halve the tomatoes, scatter them over and season with salt and pepper.

+ When you have topped the pizzas, bake each one in the oven for 8–10 minutes or until crispy and the sausage on the harissa, chilli and sausage pizza is cooked. Once cooked, scatter the arugula over. Scatter the basil leaves over the cooked goat cheese pizza and drizzle with a little oil. Drizzle the balsamic glaze over the feta pizza with a good drizzle of olive oil, then scatter over the mint leaves. Serve the pizzas immediately.

Time from start to finish:
20 minutes
Serves: 2
Equipment: Colander, blender
or food processor, medium
saucepan, large frying pan,
medium bowl or pitcher

Chilli jam

13- or 14-oz jar of mild or hot
Peppadew peppers
4 oz cherry tomatoes
½ bunch of fresh basil
6 tbsp sugar

Fritters

Sunflower oil
⅓ cup self-rising flour
¼ cup whole milk
1 egg
Salt and freshly ground black pepper
15-oz can of sweet corn
¼ cup low- or full-fat crème fraîche,
to serve

Avocado & arugula salad

1 ripe avocado
½ bag of arugula
Drizzle of extra virgin olive oil
Drizzle of balsamic vinegar
Freshly ground black pepper

Aussie sweet corn breakfast fritters with avocado & arugula salad & sweet chilli jam

Peppadew peppers, which are used in this dish, are generally found in a jar near the capers in the supermarket. However, if you can't find them, just double the cherry tomatoes, along with a bit of Tabasco.

+ First, prepare the chilli jam. Drain the Peppadew peppers well and put them in a blender or food processor with the cherry tomatoes. Rip the leaves from the basil stalks, add them too and blitz until smooth. Then transfer to a medium saucepan over a medium heat. Add the sugar and bring to the boil.

+ Meanwhile, start on the fritters. Put a big drizzle of oil into a large frying pan over a medium to high heat. Put the flour, milk and egg in a medium bowl with a big pinch of salt and some pepper. Beat the mixture hard with a wooden spoon to get rid of any lumps. Drain the sweet corn well, stir into the batter and set aside for a moment.

+ Once the chilli jam is boiling, turn down the heat and leave it to simmer away for 8 minutes, stirring it from time to time so that it does not stick to the bottom.

+ Once the oil in the frying pan is nice and hot, put four dollops of the fritter mix into the pan. Each one should be about 4 inches in diameter, which uses all of the mixture up. Cook for about 3 minutes.

+ Meanwhile, cut the avocado in half and remove the pit. The easiest way to get the pit out is to put the blade of a sharp knife into the pit as if you were going to cut it in half. Then twist the knife a bit and the pit should just pop out. Peel off the skin and slice the flesh into long, thin strips. Arrange to one side of two serving plates and set aside for a moment.

+ The underside of the fritters should now be crisp and golden brown, so flip them over and leave to cook for another 3 minutes.

>

Aussie sweet corn breakfast fritters with avocado & arugula salad & sweet chilli jam

(continued)

+ Pile the arugula into the center of each plate, drizzle with a little oil and balsamic vinegar. Once the fritters are crisp and golden on the bottom, remove them from the heat and arrange two of them on each plate opposite the avocado. Dollop the crème fraîche beside them. Remove the now-reduced chilli jam from the heat and spoon a little onto each plate. Give a little twist of black pepper over everything and serve.

+ Any remaining chilli jam can be stored in a sterilized jar in the fridge for up to one month. (See page 35 for how to sterilize jars.) It is also delicious served with meats and cheeses.

Time from start to finish:
30 minutes if making your own
tortilla chips (you actually only
save 2–3 minutes if using store-
bought!)
Serves: 4
Equipment: 1–2 large baking
sheets

Ceviche

Three 4-oz (approximately) really
fresh, skinless, sustainably caught
salmon fillets

3 green onions

¾-inch piece of fresh ginger

1–2 red chillies (depending on how
hot you like it)

1 avocado

1 dab of honey (optional: a bit of
sweetness for those with a sweet
tooth!)

1 lime

½ orange

A drizzle of extra virgin olive oil
(optional)

Salt and freshly ground black pepper

Small handful of fresh mint leaves

Tortillas

4 corn or wheat tortillas, if making
homemade tortilla chips

or

7-oz bag of tortilla chips, if not

Vegetable oil or oil spray (optional)

Salt and freshly ground black pepper

Simple salmon ceviche with tortilla chips

Use the freshest, freshest fish that you can find for
this dish. Even go to the fishmonger if you have one
near you and ask him for his finest catch. This is a
wonderfully summery South American–style dish with
lots of tang and spice. Sea bass, tuna, salmon, even
scallops can all be used here. You can either just buy
a big bag of tortilla chips or, if you fancy making your
own, they are very, very easy and I have included the
recipe below.

+ If home baking your own tortilla chips, then preheat the oven to 400°F.

+ Pull any bones from the salmon fillets and, using a sharp knife, remove
any brown flesh from underneath. Cut them up as thinly as possible (they
must be paper thin, or close to it), as if you were cutting a loaf of bread
into slices. Arrange them in a single layer on a large serving platter.

+ Trim and finely slice the onion (both the green and the white bits), peel
the ginger and chop it into thin sticks. Halve and finely slice the chillies,
discarding the seeds. Scatter all three ingredients over the salmon.

+ Halve the avocado, discard the pit and carefully peel the skin off. Then
turn each half cut side down and slice them really thinly lengthwise.
Arrange them over the salmon and drizzle the honey over, if using.

+ Squeeze the lime and orange juice over, making sure you cover all of
the fish. Drizzle with some oil, if using, and season with salt and pepper.
Cover and then leave in the fridge to "cook" for about 10 minutes.

+ If you are making tortilla chips, put the tortillas in a pile and cut them into
12 wedges as if you were cutting a cake. Lay them in a single layer on
one or two large baking sheets. Drizzle or spray with some oil, if using
(not essential but makes them a little tastier), and season with salt
and pepper.

\>

Simple salmon ceviche with tortilla chips

(continued)

+ Put the tortillas in the oven for 5 minutes. I have a habit of not remembering they are in, though, and so I really have to keep an eye on them!

+ When the tortillas are crisp and golden, remove from the oven and leave to cool for a minute before piling into a serving bowl. Or, if using store-bought tortilla chips, simply empty them into the serving bowl.

+ When the ceviche is just turning a bit white at the edges, it is ready, so remove it from the fridge. Rip up the mint leaves, scatter them over and serve with the tortilla chips.

Time from start to finish:
20 minutes
Serves: 4
Equipment: Large bowl, zester,
large frying pan, 2 baking trays

1¾ cups self-rising flour

3 tbsp soft light brown sugar

1 tsp baking powder

1 tsp ground cinnamon

2 tsp ground ginger

Pinch of salt

½ lemon

½ vanilla bean (or a couple of drops
of vanilla extract) (optional)

1 cup plus 2 tbsp low-fat milk

1 medium egg

Sunflower oil

12 slices of Parma ham (or bacon)

To serve

½ cup maple syrup

4 oz (½ cup) sour cream or low- or
full-fat crème fraîche

Gingerbread pancakes with Parma ham & maple syrup

Major brownie points are awarded to anyone who goes the extra mile on Sunday and rustles up this breakfast dish. If you prefer to have the pancakes plain, then just omit the cinnamon, ground ginger, lemon zest, vanilla and sugar; this plain mix can also be used for your Yorkshire puddings.

+ Preheat the oven to 225°F. This is to keep the ham and pancakes warm, as the pancakes are cooked in batches.

+ Put the flour, sugar, baking powder, cinnamon, ginger and salt into a large bowl, give them a quick mix and make a well in the center. Finely grate the lemon zest in. Split the vanilla bean open, scrape the seeds out and add them too (or vanilla extract, if using). Then gradually pour the milk in bit by bit, stirring all the time to give a smooth mixture. Beat the egg in well and set aside.

+ Put a drizzle of oil into a large frying pan on a medium heat and cook the Parma ham (or bacon) for 2–3 minutes on each side until nice and crisp. Then remove with tongs and drain on paper towels. Transfer to a baking tray and keep warm in the oven until ready to serve.

+ Leave the pan on the heat, but reduce the heat to low and add a little bit more oil if need be. Then spoon in four dollops of the pancake mix (to spread to about 4 inches wide). Leave to cook for 1–2 minutes until golden, then flip them over and cook for another 1–2 minutes. Slide them onto a baking tray and put in the oven to keep warm. Then repeat with the remaining mix to give 12 in total.

+ Once you have made all of the pancakes, divide them among four plates. I like to pile the Parma ham high on them, drizzle with the maple syrup and serve with a dollop of sour cream or crème fraîche.

Time from start to finish:
25 minutes
Serves: 2
Equipment: Large roasting pan,
medium saucepan

1lb baby or new potatoes

Salt and freshly ground black pepper

Olive oil

14-oz can of chopped tomatoes

4 tbsp balsamic vinegar

1–2 tsp smoked paprika

1–2 tsp sugar

5 oz or ½ cup plus 2 tbsp aïoli (store-bought, or if you fancy making your own, see page 163)

5 oz chorizo

A small handful of fresh flat leaf parsley

Roasted new patatas & chorizo bravas with aïoli

I went to a restaurant with my dad where we feasted on spicy patatas bravas, jamón ibérico that melted on the tongue like a fine butter and garlic shrimp served simply with lime and fresh herbs. My dad (the Spanish teacher) was talking to the waiter, who thought his Spanish was so good he was actually from Spain. Well, I just sat there beaming with pride. This is a recipe to remind me of that fantastic Friday lunch. There are many ways to make patatas bravas, and chorizo is not usually thrown in, but being a chorizo addict, totally entranced by its robust flavors, I just had to add some.

+ Preheat the oven to 425°F.

+ Put the potatoes into a large roasting pan. If using new potatoes (not "baby"), halve or quarter them first. Season with salt and pepper and drizzle with a good amount of oil. Roast in the hot oven for 20 minutes.

+ Pour the tomatoes into a medium saucepan over a medium heat. Add the vinegar, paprika and sugar to taste, a drizzle of oil, and salt and pepper. Bring to a simmer, then let bubble away for 15 minutes, stirring occasionally.

+ Meanwhile, make your aïoli and set aside or skip to the next step if using store-bought.

+ Peel and chop the chorizo into chunky pieces and set aside.

+ Give the sauce a stir and check on the potatoes, tossing them about a bit. Add the chorizo to the sauce for the last 5 minutes of cooking time.

+ The potatoes are cooked when crisp and golden outside and tender inside when pierced with a knife. Remove them from the oven and put on a serving platter for sharing. Take the now-reduced tomato sauce off the heat and add some salt and pepper if need be. Then pour it over the potatoes and top with the aïoli and tear over the parsley leaves. Sometimes in Spain this is served with cocktail toothpicks. Wonderful!

Time from start to finish:
35 minutes
Serves: 4
Equipment: Large saucepan,
small frying pan, immersion or
standard blender, scissors

4 tbsp butter

2 large leeks

2 large baking potatoes

½ cup white wine

1 quart good-quality chicken stock
(fresh is best to use here)

Salt and freshly ground black pepper

3 oz oak-smoked bacon pieces or
cubed pancetta

A little heavy cream (optional)

Small handful of fresh chives

Potato & leek vichyssoise with crispy bacon & chives

It has been said that this soup comes from Vichy in France, but rumor has it that the chef who created it had some Vichy roots and the link is no more than that. It is supposed to be served cold, but personally I am not one for cold potato soup. So I turned up the heat and added one of my favorite ingredients, bacon, which has been crisped up to within a very inch of its life, adding some welcome crunch and saltiness, along with a drizzle of cream and a few snips of chives.

+ Put a large saucepan on a low heat with the butter. While it is heating up, trim the leeks, remove any tough outer leaves, split them in half lengthwise and wash really well before finely slicing. Add to the pan and cook gently for about 10 minutes until really soft, stirring from time to time.

+ Meanwhile, peel and chop the potatoes into bite-size chunks. Add to the leeks (once they are cooked) along with the wine. Allow the wine to bubble down for 2–3 minutes before adding the stock and some salt and pepper. Then turn up the heat and bring to the boil. Let the soup bubble away for 10–15 minutes until the potato is nice and tender.

+ While the soup is cooking, place a small frying pan on a high heat. Once hot, add the bacon (or pancetta) pieces and fry for 3–4 minutes, stirring from time to time, until crisp and golden. Spoon onto paper towels to drain, and set aside.

+ Using an immersion blender, carefully blitz the now-cooked soup until really smooth. A standard blender does the trick also; just be careful to blend in a couple of batches.

+ Taste the soup, adding more salt and pepper if you think it needs it (but allowing for the saltiness of the bacon) and then ladle into four serving bowls. Swirl a little cream on top of each, if using, snip the chives over and finally scatter with the cooked bacon to serve.

Time from start to finish:
20 minutes
Serves: 4
Equipment: Large frying pan or
wok

Vegetable oil

1 lemongrass stalk

2 garlic cloves

2-inch piece of fresh ginger

Large handful of fresh cilantro

3 kaffir lime leaves (fresh, frozen
or dried)

Two 12-oz cans of coconut milk

1 cup plus 2 tbsp good-quality chicken
stock (fresh is best to use here)

1 red chilli

3 skinless, boneless chicken breasts

1 bunch of green onions

2 limes

2–3 tbsp fish sauce

1–2 tsp sugar

Salt and freshly ground black pepper

Thai chicken soup with coconut milk & ginger

A smoother-than-velvet Thai-style soup with an orchestra of flavors going on inside. If you can get your hands on fresh kaffir lime leaves that would be great; the dried ones can be found in the herbs and spices section in the supermarket, or use frozen.

+ Heat a drizzle of oil in a large frying pan or wok on a medium heat.

+ Trim the lemongrass stalk and discard any tough outer leaves before finely chopping the white bit (discard the green bit as it can be quite bitter). Peel and finely chop the garlic and then peel the ginger and cut it into thin slivers. Chop the stalks off the cilantro (in one go) and then finely slice them (keeping the cilantro leaves aside for later).

+ Carefully toss everything in the hot oil with the kaffir lime leaves and stir-fry for a couple of minutes, being careful that nothing sticks and burns.

+ Next add the coconut milk and stock and leave to come to the boil.

+ Meanwhile, halve the chilli lengthwise and then finely slice it, leaving the seeds in if you like it quite fiery. Chop the chicken into bite-size pieces and add both ingredients to the now-boiled soup. Reduce the heat a little and leave it to bubble away for about 8 minutes until the chicken is cooked.

+ Finely slice the onions (both the green and the white bits), juice the limes and roughly chop half of the reserved cilantro leaves. Add these once the chicken is cooked and then leave to simmer for a final minute. Last, add enough fish sauce and sugar to taste and season with salt and pepper if necessary.

+ Ladle into four serving bowls, scatter the remaining cilantro leaves over and serve.

2 cups plus 2 tbsp good-quality fish or chicken stock (fresh is best to use here)

1–2 red chillies (depending on how hot you like it)

1 lemongrass stalk

Small handful of fresh cilantro

2 kaffir lime leaves (fresh, frozen or dried)

3 tbsp fish sauce

12 sustainably caught raw jumbo shrimp, shelled

2 limes

1–2 tsp sugar

Hot-and-sour jumbo shrimp soup

A light, lucid soup with fragrant Asian flavors and succulent blushing shrimp. Definitely one for a packed lunch.

+ Pour the stock into a medium saucepan on a high heat and cover with the lid (so it heats up more quickly).

+ Meanwhile, slice, seed and finely chop the chillies and finely slice the lemongrass (the white bit only) and cilantro stalks (reserving the leaves).

+ Once the stock has come to the boil, add the cilantro stalks to the pan along with the kaffir lime leaves and fish sauce and cover again with the lid. Turn the heat down a little and leave to simmer for 4–5 minutes.

+ Add the shrimp and continue to simmer for another minute or so until they turn pink.

+ Then finish with the cilantro leaves, juice of the limes and sugar to taste.

+ Ladle into two bowls and serve.

Time from start to finish:
15 minutes
Chilling time: **30 minutes in the freezer (or 1 hour in the fridge)**
Serves: **4–6**
Equipment: **Blender or food processor, large pitcher, baking tray**

Gazpacho

2¼ lbs vine-ripened tomatoes

2 red peppers

1 garlic clove

½ bunch of fresh basil

6 tbsp extra virgin olive oil plus extra for drizzling

4 tsp sherry vinegar

A few shakes of Tabasco sauce

Pinch of sugar

Salt and freshly ground black pepper

2-inch piece of cucumber, diced

Handful of ice cubes

Croutons

1 ciabatta roll (about 3½ oz)

Extra virgin olive oil

Salt and freshly ground black pepper

Red pepper, tomato & basil gazpacho with salt & pepper croutons

Every summer I book myself and the family on Britain's favorite orange airline and head south to Spain. Circling high above Barcelona's La Rambla, which leads down to the sparkling sapphire blue surf, I know that very soon I will be among the bustling throng of beautiful bronzed bodies, sipping a bubbling cava, dipping hunks of just-cooked bread in hot sizzling oil full of garlicky shrimp and diving my spoon into a perfect bowl of that intensely flavored, cooling Spanish soup.

+ Preheat the oven to 400°F.

+ Roughly chop the tomatoes, halve and seed the peppers, snapping them into a few pieces, and peel the garlic. Pick the leaves from the basil stalks, reserve a small handful for garnish and put the rest in a blender or food processor with the tomatoes, peppers and garlic. Then add the oil, sherry vinegar, Tabasco, sugar and some salt and pepper and blitz until as smooth as possible.

+ Taste, adding a little more Tabasco or seasoning if you think it needs it. Pour into a large, sturdy pitcher, cover with plastic wrap and put in the freezer for 30 minutes (or the fridge for 1 hour) to cool right down.

+ Cut the ciabatta up into bite-sized cubes, scatter them on a baking tray, drizzle with oil and season with salt and pepper. Bake in the oven for about 6 minutes.

+ Remove the croutons from the oven once they are crisp and golden and set aside until ready to serve.

+ When ready to serve, divide the soup among the serving bowls. Sprinkle the cucumber over, pop a few ice cubes in each one, scatter the croutons and reserved basil on top and drizzle with a little oil.

Broccoli & blue cheese soup with chive mascarpone & warm garlic bread

Time from start to finish:
30 minutes
Serves: 6
Equipment: Large saucepan with lid, 2 small bowls, baking tray, blender

Soup

Vegetable oil

1 large leek

1 large potato

½ cup good-quality chicken stock (fresh is best to use here)

1 whole head of broccoli

5 oz strong blue cheese, such as Stilton or Roquefort

Salt and freshly ground black pepper

Accompaniments

3 garlic cloves

Small handful of fresh chives

¼ cup softened butter

Salt and freshly ground black pepper

1 French baguette

6 tbsp mascarpone

Roquefort is the cheese to go for if you like this superstrong, or you can keep it British with some good old Stilton. Either way, I really like the combination of a blue cheese with some broccoli—definitely one of my top 10 favorite flavor combos. A lovely, filling winter soup.

+ Put a drizzle of oil into a large saucepan or pot over a medium heat and while this heats up, trim the leek, discarding most of the dark green bit. Then slit it lengthwise, discard the hard outer leaves and wash well under the cold tap. Finely slice and add to the pan, then give a stir and leave to cook for about 10 minutes.

+ Meanwhile, prepare the garlic butter. Peel and finely chop the garlic and finely chop the chives. Put all of the garlic and half of the chives into a small bowl with the softened butter and some salt and pepper. Mix and set aside.

+ Returning to the soup, peel and chop the potato into ¼-inch cubes and add to the softened leeks, along with the chicken stock. Turn up the heat and put the lid on to help bring it up to the boil quickly.

+ Once this is boiling remove the lid, reduce the heat a little and leave to simmer away for 10 minutes or so.

+ Preheat the oven to 350°F for the garlic bread.

+ Roughly chop the broccoli (including the stalk) and add to the soup for the last 5 minutes or so.

+ Now, divide the baguette into three even-sized pieces and split each one in half as if you were making a sandwich. Pop the bread, cut side up, on

>

Broccoli & blue cheese soup with chive mascarpone & warm garlic bread

(continued)

a baking tray and put in the oven for 5 minutes. (I have to really keep an eye on it as I sometimes don't remember that it is in there!)

+ Meanwhile, put the remaining chives in a small bowl with the mascarpone. Season with salt and pepper and stir together once (otherwise it might go grainy), then set aside.

+ Remove the toasted bread from the oven, slather the cut sides with the garlic butter and return it to the oven for a further 4–5 minutes.

+ Once the soup is ready, check that the potatoes and broccoli are cooked through and remove from the heat. Carefully blitz the soup in the blender until smooth. Crumble in the blue cheese, give the soup another quick blitz and then season to taste.

+ Divide the soup among six serving bowls. Add a dollop of the chive mascarpone to each. Remove the garlic bread from the oven and serve a piece with each serving.

Time from start to finish:
40 minutes
Serves: 4
Equipment: Large saucepan with lid, food processor fitted with the slicing blade attachment (optional), baking sheet, grater

Soup

Vegetable oil

Pat of butter

4 big onions

1 bay leaf

2 garlic cloves

Small handful of fresh sage leaves

1 tbsp all-purpose flour

1 quart good-quality beef stock

Salt and freshly ground black pepper

Small handful of fresh flat leaf parsley

Croutons

1 small baguette

3 oz Gruyère cheese (Parmesan works well too)

Big pinch of English mustard powder

French onion & sage soup with big fat Gruyère & mustard croutons

I really do love a good bowl of French onion soup. Of course the best soups are made with the very best stock: a rich, thick beef stock that has been cooked for hours, so deep in flavor I could do a little dance. This is best made with a fresh stock from the butcher, but a supermarket one (not from concentrate) will do just fine too. I sometimes hold the cooked soup in a thermos to have when I am on the go. A lovely luscious lunchtime treat.

+ Place a large saucepan or pot on a medium heat with a drizzle of oil and the butter. Peel and very finely slice the onions. This is a bit of a task, but using a food processor fitted with the slicing blade attachment should make things a bit easier.

+ Add the onions to the pan with the bay leaf, pop the lid on and leave to cook for about 25 minutes until soft. Give them a good stir every now and then so they don't burn. If they look like they are sticking at any time, just add a little more oil.

+ Meanwhile, peel and finely chop the garlic, then finely chop the sage leaves and set both aside.

+ Preheat the oven to 300°F. Trim the baguette ends, cut it into eight thick slices (about 1 inch thick) and lay them out on a baking sheet.

+ Next, roughly grate the Gruyère cheese (or Parmesan), sprinkle the mustard powder over, and toss it all about to mix together. Then spread it evenly over the tops of the bread slices.

+ Check on the onions, giving them a good stir every now and then.

>

French onion & sage soup with big fat Gruyère & mustard croutons

(continued)

+ Once the onions are a few minutes from being ready, place the croutons in the oven to bake for 4–5 minutes. You could also broil them for about 5 minutes if you prefer.

+ Once the onions are lovely and soft, add the garlic, sage and flour, giving them a good stir in. Pour in the beef stock, put the lid back on, increase the heat and bring the soup up to the boil. Then leave it to bubble away for 2–3 minutes before removing it from the heat. Season to taste with salt and pepper.

+ Remove the crisp, melted-cheese-topped croutons from the oven. Pick and roughly chop the parsley leaves.

+ Divide the soup among four wide bowls and serve with the croutons either sitting right on top of the soup or to the side of the bowl. Scatter the parsley over and serve.

Salads

I am easily satisfied with the very best.
Winston Churchill

I remember when a salad used to be a not-so-pretty-looking piece of iceberg lettuce, a few slivers of cucumber with a plump, round tomato quartered and scattered on top. Oh, how things have moved on! There is an incredible array of salad leaves, veg and even fruit now available since those heady days of big Afros and flared trousers, and in order to counterbalance my penchant for all things sweet, I tend to whip up a fast and fresh salad several times a week.

Time from start to finish:
20 minutes
Serves: 4
Equipment: Large serving platter

Two 9-oz packages of prepared mango cubes (or 2 large ripe mangoes)

7 oz feta cheese

4 radishes

1 ripe avocado

Small handful of fresh basil

1 bag of pea shoots (or wild arugula)

Salt and freshly ground black pepper

A drizzle of a really good extra virgin olive oil

1 lime

Mango, feta & avocado salad with fresh lime juice

Mangoes are not the cheapest things to buy, nor is their comrade the avocado. But once in a while, a tasty tropical treat is a necessity for me. In one of the many places that I love, Sri Lanka, the avocados grow in abundance. Early in the morning, I would wake up, grab my friend and stand ready under the avo tree. After a gentle shake, dozens of these emerald green fruits would come tumbling to the ground. Sitting in my kitchen back in London with the holiday blues, I devised this recipe as a way of transporting me back to the exotic, calming world that is Sri Lanka's southern coast. I found the pea shoots in the supermarket near me—they are little baby leaves, very cute and tasty. If you can't find them, wild arugula is fine to use instead.

+ Put the mango onto a large serving platter. (I do love some prepared mango at times!) Or if using whole mangoes, slice the two cheeks off either side of the pit. Cut them in half and then run the knife through the flesh close to the skin to peel it, as you would with a melon. Dice the flesh into bite-size pieces and scatter onto the big serving platter. I like to go back and slice off the remaining skinny bits of mango and do the same thing with them so as not to waste any.

+ Crumble the feta cheese over. Trim the radishes and then slice them as fine as you can before scattering them over also.

+ Cut the avocado in half and discard the pit. I put the blade of a knife into it and then give it a twist—the pit usually comes out beautifully. Then carefully peel away the skin and slice or dice up the avocado and add to the salad.

+ Tear the basil leaves from the stalks and scatter the leaves over with the pea shoots (or arugula). Season with salt and pepper, drizzle with oil and finish by squeezing the lime juice over.

Time from start to finish:
20 minutes
Serves: 2
Equipment: Small frying pan,
small bowl, small plate

2 oz walnut pieces

5 oz seedless red grapes

2 celery sticks

2 Granny Smith apples

Small handful of fresh flat leaf parsley
or dill

2 oz dried cranberries (or raisins)

Dressing

4 oz (½ cup) Greek yogurt (full-fat,
low-fat or no-fat)

1–2 tsp honey

1 tsp Dijon mustard

Salt and freshly ground black pepper

Wild Waldorf salad with toasted walnuts & Granny Smiths

I am not sure why I named this salad "wild"; it must have been my frame of mind at the time or perhaps I was just in search of a suitable alliteration! I always double up this recipe so I can have it throughout the week as a packed lunch, or it's delicious served with some pan-fried chicken. I usually take a skinless, boneless chicken breast, bash it until it's very thin, squish it in some thyme, salt and pepper and then fry until cooked. I leave the chicken to cool, then pop it on top of my wild Waldorf salad in my plastic lunch box.

+ Put a small frying pan on a low to medium heat, with no oil, for the walnuts. While waiting for that to heat up, get on with the dressing.

+ Spoon the Greek yogurt into a small bowl and add the honey (to taste) and Dijon mustard. Mix them together well, season to taste with salt and pepper and set aside.

+ Put the walnuts in the now-hot pan and leave to toast for 2–3 minutes, tossing them about occasionally so they don't burn.

+ Meanwhile, wash and halve the grapes, finely slice the celery and throw them into a medium serving bowl.

+ Remove the walnuts from the heat and transfer to a small plate to stop them from toasting further. Leave them to cool down for a bit.

+ Quarter the apples, remove their cores, chop them into bite-size chunks and add them to the serving bowl. Then pick and roughly chop the parsley or dill leaves and throw them in along with the cranberries (or raisins). Then add the walnuts, crumbling any that are large.

+ Add the dressing to the salad, toss everything together, season to taste, adding a little more honey, herbs or salt and pepper if you think it needs it, and serve.

Time from start to finish:
20 minutes
Serves: 4–6
Equipment: Kettle, mug or small
bowl, zester, colander, medium
saucepan, peeler

14-oz can of cannellini beans

Pinch of salt

9-oz bunch of asparagus

3 zucchini

1 perfectly ripe avocado

Olive oil

1 bag of wild arugula

Small handful of fresh mint

Small handful of fresh basil

Handful of toasted pine nuts (about
1 oz) (they come ready-toasted from
the supermarket)

1 oz Parmesan cheese

Dressing

1 small red chilli or a pinch of dried
chilli flakes (optional)

1 lemon

4 tbsp extra virgin olive oil

Couple of squeezes or dabs of honey

Salt and freshly ground black pepper

Zucchini "pappardelle" with asparagus, avocado salad & arugula

A lovely, light on-the-go lunch that will become the envy of your colleagues, or a simple, inviting supper dish.

+ Put the kettle on to boil.

+ Meanwhile, make the dressing. Seed and finely chop the chilli (if using) and add to a mug or small bowl, or simply add the dried chilli flakes. Finely grate the lemon zest in and squeeze in the juice. Add the oil and honey and season with salt and pepper. Whisk together with a fork. Next, drain and rinse the cannellini beans, toss them through the dressing and set aside.

+ Pour the now-boiled water and a big pinch of salt into a medium saucepan and put on a high heat to bring the water back up to the boil. Trim the ends off the asparagus where they look dried out and add the spears to the water to cook for 4 minutes.

+ Using a peeler, take a strip off the length of a zucchini to look like pappardelle. Keep going in the same place until you have peeled away half of the zucchini, then flip it over and do the same with the other side. You now don't need the bit that is left when you've peeled away all you can, but you could save it for use in a soup or stir-fry. Repeat with the remaining zucchini.

+ Once the asparagus is just tender, remove it from the water with a slotted spoon and rinse under cold running water for a minute or so until cool. Then set aside. Now add the zucchini "pappardelle" to the boiling water and cook for about 3 minutes.

+ Meanwhile, quarter, pit and peel the avocado. Cut it lengthwise into ¼-inch-thick slices, drizzle with oil (so they don't go brown) and set aside.

+ Once the zucchini are just tender, drain them in the colander and rinse under cold running water until cool. Drain well and toss a drizzle of oil through to stop them from sticking together.

>

Zucchini "pappardelle" with asparagus, avocado salad & arugula

(continued)

+ Now to assemble. Put the arugula onto a large serving platter. Scatter the zucchini and asparagus over. Rip the leaves from the mint and basil stalks and sprinkle them over with the pine nuts. Give everything a little toss about with your hands and then arrange the avocado on top. Spoon the cannellini beans and dressing over and then shave the Parmesan on top using the peeler and serve.

Time from start to finish:
20 minutes
Serves: 4
Equipment: Large frying pan,
small bowl, colander, large bowl,
large plate, pestle and mortar
(or mug and rolling pin)

Vegetable oil

4 rump or sirloin steaks, about ¾ inch
thick (about 1¼ lbs in total)

Salt and freshly ground black pepper

1 head of romaine lettuce

Large handful of fresh cilantro

Large handful of fresh mint

Small handful of fresh basil

2 oz salted, roasted peanuts (not dry
roasted)

Dressing

1 hot red chilli

¾-inch piece of fresh ginger

1 garlic clove

2 large or 3 small limes

2 tbsp vegetable oil

1 tbsp fish sauce

Large squeeze or dab of honey

Salt and freshly ground black pepper

Thai beef salad with roasted peanuts & chilli dressing

A supereasy, supersimple and, dare I say it, pretty healthy salad. Great for those last days of summer or for a light autumnal meal. I like to use rump steak, but sirloin or even fillet, if you are going for it, will do.

+ Put a large frying pan on a high heat with a drizzle of oil. Season the steaks well with a good amount of salt and pepper. This will give the steaks a tasty crust once cooked. Add them to the hot oil and leave to cook, untouched, for 3–4 minutes, depending on how well you like them done.

+ Meanwhile, get on with the dressing. Halve and seed the chilli, peel the ginger and garlic and then finely chop everything. Place in a small bowl and squeeze the lime juice over. Add the oil, fish sauce and honey, beat together with a fork, season with salt and pepper to taste and then leave to infuse.

+ Once the steaks have cooked for 3–4 minutes, flip them over and cook for another 3–4 minutes while you prepare the salad.

+ Trim the end off the romaine lettuce, separate the leaves and discard the very center. Put in a colander, rinse well and then gently pat dry with paper towels. Stack the leaves together and then cut into about ¼-inch-thick slices and place in a large bowl.

+ Bunch the cilantro, mint and basil together, rip off the leafy tops and add to the bowl also. (I keep stalks for stocks and soups. They freeze really well and can be used straight from frozen.)

+ Remove the now-cooked steaks from the pan and leave to rest on a large plate, loosely covered with aluminum foil, for about 5 minutes.

+ Meanwhile, roughly grind the peanuts with a pestle and mortar and set aside. Alternatively, just put them in a mug and use the end of a rolling pin to crush them.

>

Thai beef salad
with roasted peanuts
& chilli dressing

(continued)

+ Pour half of the dressing onto the salad leaves and toss together well. Then divide them among four serving plates. Take half of the nuts and sprinkle them over the salads.

+ Remove the fat from the steaks and then cut the meat into slices about ¼ inch thick. Arrange them on top of the salads, sprinkle with the remaining nuts, drizzle with the rest of the dressing and then serve.

Time from start to finish:
15 minutes
Serves: 4
Equipment: Small saucepan,
baking sheet, mini blender,
grater, colander, really large
bowl, small frying pan

4 medium eggs

¼ French baguette

Extra virgin olive oil

Salt and freshly ground black pepper

Two 12-oz romaine lettuce heads

½ lb sustainably caught raw peeled shrimp

2 tbsp pomegranate seeds (optional, you can find them prepared at the supermarket)

Dressing

1 garlic clove

1 scant oz Parmesan cheese

8 tbsp mayonnaise

3 anchovies (the sort that come in cans or jars)

½ lime

Salt and freshly ground black pepper

Shrimp Caesar salad with olive oil croutons & pomegranate seeds

A very scrumptious salad. Sometimes I like to put all of the salad (undressed) in a plastic container and take the dressing in a separate small one. A really good alternative to sandwiches in the middle of the day or a lighter bite for dinner.

+ Turn the oven on to 400°F.

+ Place the eggs in a small pan and cover with water. Put on a high heat and as soon as the water comes to the boil, let it bubble away for 4 minutes for almost hard-boiled eggs.

+ Cut the baguette into approximately ¾-inch-square croutons, toss them on a baking sheet, drizzle generously with oil and pop them into the oven for about 6 minutes.

+ Meanwhile, peel and roughly chop the garlic and place in a mini blender. Finely grate the Parmesan and add it along with the mayonnaise and anchovies, then squeeze in the lime juice. Whiz until really smooth and creamy, season with salt and pepper to taste and set aside.

+ Toss the croutons about a bit and return for the remaining cooking time (if not already done).

+ As soon as the eggs are ready, drain them in a colander and run cold water over them for a couple of minutes to stop them cooking.

+ Meanwhile, trim the ends off the lettuces, wash and pat the leaves dry with paper towels or a clean tea towel and then rip them up into big pieces and put in a really large bowl.

+ Put a drizzle of oil in a small frying pan on a low heat.

+ Peel the cooled eggs, quarter them and set aside.

+ The croutons should now be crisp and golden, so remove them from the oven and set aside.

>

Shrimp Caesar salad with olive oil croutons & pomegranate seeds

(continued)

+ Turn the heat up to high under the frying pan and add the shrimp, season well with salt and pepper and cook for 2–3 minutes until they turn pink and are cooked through.

+ Finally, pour the dressing all over the lettuce and toss gently using two large spoons. Divide among the serving plates, then spoon the shrimp over, nestle the egg wedges around, scatter the croutons on top with the pomegranate seeds, if using, and serve.

Time from start to finish:
20 minutes
Serves: 4
Equipment: Kettle, mug or
small bowl, medium saucepan,
colander, small bowl

11 oz baby or new potatoes

4-oz bag of salad leaves, like spinach
or mâche

1 head of chicory

9-oz package of cooked beets (comes
in a vac pack from the fruit and veg
section of the supermarket)

2 oz (¼ cup) capers

1 Granny Smith apple

½ lime

11-oz package of hot-smoked mackerel
(with or without peppercorns)

2 oz roasted hazelnuts (available from
supermarkets ready roasted)

Freshly ground black pepper

Dressing

Small handful of fresh dill

4 tbsp horseradish sauce

2 tbsp low- or full-fat crème fraîche

1 lime

Squeeze or dab of honey (optional)

Salt and freshly ground black pepper

Mackerel salad with horseradish crème fraîche

One of my favorite foods, which I love served whole, is mackerel. Its opalescent skin slashed, the fresh fish lightly grilled and then served with a tart gooseberry sauce; or smoked mackerel in a salad, straight from the package. A large dollop of horseradish sauce can stand up to this intensely flavored fish with some tart Granny Smith apples to cut through its inviting fattiness.

+ Put the kettle on to boil.

+ Meanwhile, make the dressing for the salad. Pick and finely chop the dill leaves and add half to a mug or small bowl (reserving the rest for later). Mix in the horseradish sauce, crème fraîche, enough lime juice to taste and honey (if using). Season to taste with salt and pepper and set aside.

+ Wash the potatoes, put in a medium saucepan over a high heat with a little salt and cover with the now-boiled water. Leave to bubble away for about 15 minutes.

+ Put the salad leaves on each of four serving plates or one large serving platter. Trim the end off the chicory, separate the leaves and scatter them over, discarding any damaged outer leaves.

+ Drain the beets and cut into small wedges. Rinse and drain the capers. Quarter and core the apple and then slice it into matchsticks. Toss it in a small bowl with the lime juice and then scatter it over the leaves with the beets and capers.

+ Peel the skin from the back of the mackerel, remove the dark brown meat and then break the flesh into large chunks and arrange on top of the salad.

+ Check that the potatoes are now tender, then drain them well and leave to cool for a moment.

+ Roughly chop the hazelnuts and scatter over the salad. Nestle the potatoes in now also. Drizzle the dressing back and forth over the salad, scatter the remaining dill on top with a twist of black pepper and serve.

Time from start to finish:
20 minutes
Serves: 4
Equipment: Small saucepan,
colander, mug or small bowl,
peeler

4 medium eggs

2 bags of spinach and arugula salad

½ small red onion

½ cucumber

2 handfuls of pitted black olives (about 4 oz)

14-oz can of lima beans

7 oz sundried (or sun blush) tomatoes

4 hot-smoked trout fillets (or smoked mackerel fillets, steamed salmon fillets or hot-smoked salmon fillets)

1 oz Parmesan cheese (optional)

A few sprigs of fresh dill

Dressing

4 tbsp extra virgin olive oil

2 tbsp white wine vinegar (balsamic will also work)

A tiny squeeze or dab of honey (optional)

Pinch of English mustard powder

Salt and freshly ground black pepper

Nifty Niçoise salad with hot-smoked trout & sundried tomatoes

The first time I spotted this on the menu, I asked what was the salad "Nic-o-ez." After a look of pity, a raised eyebrow and a helping hand with the correct pronunciation, I dived into my very first salade Niçoise. I have adapted the traditional recipe, adding some abundantly flavored trout and doing away with the ever-present potatoes in favor of some creamy lima beans.

+ Place the eggs in a small saucepan and cover with water. Put on a high heat and as soon as the water comes to the boil, let it bubble away for 4 minutes for almost hard-boiled eggs.

+ Meanwhile, divide the salad leaves among four serving plates. Peel and finely slice the red onion, slice up the cucumber and scatter these over the salad leaves along with the olives.

+ Drain and rinse the lima beans well, halve the sundried (or sun blush) tomatoes and arrange these on top also.

+ As soon as the eggs have had their cooking time, drain in the colander and run cold water over them for a couple of minutes to stop them cooking further.

+ Meanwhile, make the dressing for the salad. Put the oil, vinegar, honey, if using, mustard powder and some salt and pepper in a mug or small bowl. Mix together with a fork and set aside.

+ Peel and quarter the cooled eggs and arrange them on the salad. Either lay the smoked fish fillets on whole or break them into pieces over each salad. Drizzle the dressing over, shave the Parmesan on top using a peeler, rip up the dill, scatter over, then serve, looking out for any small bones in the trout.

Time from start to finish:
15 minutes
Serves: 4
Equipment: Colander, scissors

14-oz can of kidney beans

7 oz cherry tomatoes

2 ready-cooked chicken breasts

2-oz package of precooked bacon

5 oz blue cheese

1 ripe avocado

Olive oil

1 lime

9-oz package of ready-prepared
mango cubes

Salt and freshly ground black pepper

The Union cobb

For the ease of making this salad, I have used ingredients that are precooked and prepackaged. Of course, if you are not a fan of those kinds of supermarket products, then cook the chicken breasts and the bacon yourself. For an impromptu dish that I have found really does impress, then it's ready-to-go products for me, but when time permits, I make everything from scratch. The ingredients below are my favorite for a cobb, but if you fancy something different, just go ahead and throw it in.

+ First, prepare all the ingredients, keeping them separate as you go. Drain and rinse the kidney beans. Halve the tomatoes and cut the chicken breasts into small bite-size chunks. Use scissors to snip the crispy bacon into small pieces. Crumble the blue cheese. Halve the avocado, remove the pit, peel off the skin and dice the flesh into cubes, then drizzle them with a little bit of oil or squeeze some lime juice over so they do not go brown and now we are ready to go.

+ Arrange the ingredients (including the already prepared mango) in whichever way tickles your fancy. I like to create a British flag (very patriotic!), but you could arrange them in stripes or rings or layered up in a jar, for example. Even putting everything in a bowl and tossing it all together works too. Then squeeze over more lime juice, drizzle with oil, season with salt and pepper and serve.

Chicken + duck mains

Laughter is brightest where food is best.
Irish proverb

My mealtime fallback seems to be chicken. A dash to
the local supermarket to grab some chicken breasts
or thighs off the shelves, then a quick rush home to
whip something up. I used to just prepare the same
repertoire of meals, the same old failsafes that I always
make without thinking. Those dishes and family favorites
are great and serve an important purpose, but I really
wanted to try and add to that repertoire to give people
even more variety for their daily meals. The good thing
with poultry is that it can take lots of flavor, so when I
am testing with it, I can have lots of fun, adding a touch
of spice here or a bit of tang there, mixing it all up with
layers of flavors.

Whole roast perky peri peri chicken

Prep time (before and after cooking): 30 minutes
Time roasting in the oven:
1 hour 50 minutes (depending on the size of bird)
Serves: 4
Equipment: Large roasting pan, small bowl, grater, large plate, medium ovenproof dish, mug or small bowl

4¼-lb whole chicken, preferably free range and/or organic
Salt and freshly ground black pepper
Olive oil
⅔ cup water, chicken stock or red wine

Peri peri sauce

5 garlic cloves
1–5 red chillies (as hot as you dare!)
¾-inch piece of fresh ginger
¼ cup vegetable oil
2 tbsp white or red wine vinegar
3 tbsp soy sauce
1–2 tbsp Tabasco sauce (again, as hot as you dare!)
2 tbsp smoked paprika
3 tsp dried oregano
1 tsp sugar (optional)
1 lime

Vegetables

3 red onions
1 lb baby or new potatoes

Salad

1 lime
1 tsp sugar (or a dab of honey)
3 tbsp extra virgin olive oil
Salt and freshly ground black pepper
1 bag of crisp salad leaves

A different way to roast chicken. A 3¼–3½-lb chicken would be about enough to serve four people, but I have given the recipe a bigger bird so that there is some meat left over for sandwiches the next day. If you use a different size from the one here, work out the cooking time based on 20 minutes per pound, plus 20 minutes. Regardless of what size bird you use, add the onions and potatoes about 45 minutes before the end of the cooking time. To speed up the cooking process, use some good sharp scissors to snip the chicken along the backbone to splay it out and cook flat.

+ Preheat the oven to 400°F. Sit the chicken in a large roasting pan and season well with salt and pepper and drizzle with oil. Place in the oven and cook for 1 hour, and meanwhile prepare the peri peri sauce.

+ Peel and roughly chop the garlic, halve, seed and finely chop the chillies and place both in a small bowl. Finely grate in the ginger (unpeeled) and then add the oil, vinegar, soy sauce, Tabasco, smoked paprika, oregano and sugar (if using). Finely grate in the lime zest and then squeeze in the juice and mix together.

+ Remove the chicken from the oven after 1 hour and spoon or pour three-quarters of the peri peri sauce onto it, spreading it all over with the back of a spoon. Peel and quarter the onions, leaving the roots intact, and toss them in around the chicken along with the potatoes. Season them with salt and pepper and then return to the oven to cook for the final 50 or so minutes. At the end of the cooking time the chicken will most likely look burned, but worry not, as this is the peri peri style.

>

Whole roast perky peri peri chicken

(continued)

+ To check that the chicken is cooked, pierce the thickest part of a thigh with the point of a sharp knife and the juices should run clear. Check that the meat has no pinkness remaining and that it is completely cooked through. Once cooked, carefully lift the chicken from the roasting pan onto a large plate and cover it loosely with aluminum foil so it can rest and become juicier. Using a slotted spoon, remove the vegetables from the pan also, transferring them to a medium ovenproof dish. Then put them back in the oven (with the oven now turned off) to keep warm.

+ Carefully pour the oil out of the roasting pan, leaving the juices and sticky bits behind. Put it on a medium heat and add the remaining sauce and 2/3 cup of water, stock or red wine. Allow to simmer for a few minutes, scraping up all the sticky bits from the bottom.

+ Meanwhile, prepare the salad. Squeeze the lime juice into a mug or small bowl and add the sugar (or honey), oil and a little salt and pepper. Give it a good whisk up. Put the salad leaves into a large salad bowl, pour the dressing over and toss the leaves about.

+ Returning to the chicken, pour any juices from the plate into the sauce before carving the meat up. Arrange on serving plates with the roasted onions and potatoes. Serve with the dressed salad and the sauce in a small pitcher.

Time from start to finish:
20 minutes
Serves: 4
Equipment: Kettle, medium
sauté pan, small bowl, medium
saucepan with tight-fitting lid,
scissors

Rice

4 oz cashew nuts (not roasted or salted)

2 cups basmati rice

2 tsp mild, medium or hot curry powder (depending on how hot you like it)

4 oz frozen peas

Salt and freshly ground black pepper

Curry

2 tbsp mild, medium or hot curry powder (depending on how hot you like it)

2 tsp garam masala (easy to find in the supermarket)

1 tsp ground cinnamon

¼ tsp ground ginger

1–3 tsp medium chilli powder (depending on how hot you like it)

4 skinless, boneless chicken breasts

Salt and freshly ground black pepper

Vegetable oil

12-oz can of coconut milk

¾ cup water

1 bunch of green onions

1 garlic clove

1 tsp sugar (optional)

Small handful of fresh cilantro

Really simple Sri Lankan chicken curry with coconut milk & cashew nut rice

I do love an Indian curry—in fact I love a curry of any description—but Sri Lankans also know how to make a good curried dish. Nestled in the southeast of southern India, just a stone's throw from the Maldives, lies a place very close to my heart, somewhere I visit often. Formerly known as Ceylon, Sri Lanka really is a feast for the senses: bright colors, vibrant flavors, wonderful beaches and people. Much of my cooking is influenced by this beautiful island, and this is my favorite Sri Lankan chicken curry. Use a thick, full-fat coconut milk for a nice creamy sauce.

+ Put the kettle on to boil for the rice.

+ While waiting, put a medium sauté pan on a high heat and throw in the cashew nuts (without any oil). Cook for 3–4 minutes, tossing from time to time, until golden. Put in a small bowl and set aside. Leave the dry pan on a low heat for the curry.

+ Once the kettle has boiled, put the rice, curry powder and a little salt into a medium saucepan and pour the boiled water over so it comes about ¾ inch above the top of the rice (this is approximately 2 cups). Cover with the lid and return to the boil. Then reduce the heat to really low and cook for as long as it says on the package. Set the timer for halfway through as you will be adding more ingredients then.

+ Now for the curry. To the hot pan (without any oil), add the curry powder, garam masala, cinnamon, ginger and chilli powder and cook for 2–3 minutes, or until you start to really smell the spices, tossing regularly.

\>

Really simple Sri Lankan chicken curry with coconut milk & cashew nut rice

(continued)

+ While they toast, snip the chicken into big bite-size chunks with scissors and season them well with salt and pepper. Pour a good drizzle of oil into the spice pan and turn the heat up to high. Add the chicken and cook for 2–3 minutes, tossing the pieces from time to time so they brown all over.

+ By this stage the rice will be about halfway through cooking. Scatter the toasted cashew nuts and peas on top, without stirring them in, and put the lid back on for the remaining 5 minutes of cooking time.

+ Going back to the curry, remove the pan from the heat while you pour the coconut milk in along with the water. Return it to the stove, turn up the heat and let it bubble away for a few minutes.

+ Meanwhile, trim and finely chop the green onions (both the green and the white bits) and peel and finely chop the garlic. Add them to the curry and leave to cook for 2–3 minutes, reducing the heat if bubbling too hard and giving it a stir from time to time.

+ Once the rice is cooked, turn off the heat, season with salt and pepper and then put the lid back on to keep the rice warm.

+ Check that the chicken is cooked by piercing with a knife—there should be no pinkness remaining. Then have a taste of the curry, adjusting the seasoning and adding the sugar if desired. Divide the rice among four plates, top with the curry, tear the cilantro leaves over and serve.

Time from start to finish:
40 minutes
Serves: 4
Equipment: Large roasting pan,
2 medium bowls, zester,
colander, kettle, medium
saucepan with lid, grater

Chicken

1 onion

3 garlic cloves

4 large chicken legs or breasts on
the bone or 8 thigh pieces on the
bone (you can use boneless chicken
pieces also) or a mix of 16 wings and
drumsticks

3 tbsp balsamic vinegar

1–4 tbsp Tabasco sauce (as hot as you
dare!)

1 tbsp soft light brown sugar

2 tsp ground allspice

2 tsp English mustard powder

1 tsp ground cinnamon

A few shakes of soy sauce

1 lime

½ orange

A few fresh thyme sprigs

Salt and freshly ground black pepper

Pineapple salsa

½ large pineapple or 14 oz prepared
fresh pineapple chunks

6 cherry tomatoes

Small handful of fresh cilantro

1 lime

Salt and freshly ground black pepper

Rice and beans

14-oz can of kidney beans

Small handful of fresh cilantro or flat
leaf parsley

2 cups instant long-grain rice

1½ cups of coconut milk

¾-inch piece of fresh ginger

1 red chilli

Baked jerk chicken with pineapple salsa, coconut rice & beans

This may not seem like the shortest list of ingredients
you have ever happened across, but upon close
inspection, you'll see they are very easy to get. This
recipe forms part of my Jamaican-St. Lucian-Bajan-
English-Polish roots. There may be some liquid left
in the roasting pan after the cooking time—this is
wonderful drizzled on the chicken to serve.

+ Preheat the oven to 400°F.

+ Peel the onion, cut it into wedges and then bash the garlic cloves
  open with the side of a knife. Toss them into a large roasting pan with
  the chicken pieces and set aside.

+ Now make up the sauce in a medium bowl. Put the balsamic vinegar,
  Tabasco, sugar, allspice, mustard powder, cinnamon and soy sauce into
  the bowl. Squeeze in the juice from the lime, finely grate the zest from the
  orange and squeeze its juice over too. Run your fingers down the length
  of the thyme sprigs to release the leaves and toss them in also. Season
  with salt and pepper, mix together and pour half over the chicken.
  Toss to coat, lay the pieces in a single layer and roast in the oven for
  30 minutes.

+ Meanwhile, make the pineapple salsa. Peel, core and finely chop the
  pineapple, or chop the pineapple chunks into smaller cubes with a
  serrated knife. Quarter the cherry tomatoes and pick and roughly chop
  the cilantro leaves. Toss them in a medium bowl with the juice from the
  lime, season to taste with salt and pepper and set aside.

+ Next drain and rinse the kidney beans for the rice and pick and roughly
  chop the cilantro or parsley leaves for the garnish, reserving both for later.

+ Put the kettle on to boil for the rice. Put the rice in a medium saucepan over
  a high heat and add the coconut milk. Leave this to come to the boil.

>

Baked jerk chicken with pineapple salsa, coconut rice & beans

(continued)

+ Meanwhile, peel and finely grate the ginger and halve, seed and finely chop the chilli. Once the coconut milk is boiling, add the ginger and chilli to it with enough boiled water so that all the liquid comes over the rice by about ¾ inch (roughly ¾ cup of water). Turn down the heat to low, put the lid on and cook for as long as it says on the package. The beans need to be added 5 minutes before the rice is ready, so set your timer accordingly.

+ The chicken should be about halfway through cooking, so pour the remaining sauce over the chicken to baste.

+ When the rice has just 5 minutes left to cook, add the kidney beans (without stirring them in), put the lid back on and leave to finish cooking.

+ Once the cooking time is up, check that the chicken is cooked by piercing it with a knife. There should be no pinkness in the meat.

+ Fluff up the now-cooked rice, gently stirring the kidney beans through, and divide among four serving plates. Sit the chicken and onion pieces on top and spoon the sauce over. Spoon the salsa to the side, scatter the chopped cilantro or parsley over and serve.

Time from start to finish:
45 minutes
Serves: 4
Equipment: Large roasting pan,
small bowl, kettle, large bowl,
medium saucepan with lid,
colander

1¾ lbs mixed chicken wings and
drumsticks

Sauce

6 squeezes or dabs of tomato ketchup

3 tbsp balsamic vinegar

3 tbsp soy sauce

2 tbsp Chinese five-spice powder

2 squeezes or dabs of honey

1 garlic clove

A few sprigs of fresh thyme

Salt and freshly ground black pepper

Sunflower oil

Slaw

¼ head of red cabbage

1 small red onion

1 small red chilli

1 big handful of raisins (about 1 oz)

Pinch of English mustard powder
(optional)

2 squeezes or dabs of honey

5 tbsp Greek yogurt (full-fat, low-fat
or no-fat)

1 lime

Salt and freshly ground black pepper

Corn rice

2 cups instant long grain-rice

7-oz can of sweet corn

Salt and freshly ground black pepper

Sunflower oil

1-oz (approximately) bunch of fresh
cilantro or flat leaf parsley

Sticky Asian BBQ chicken wings with sweet corn rice & red cabbage slaw

If the weather permits, cook the chicken on the grill for that smoky, woody, charcoal flavor. If not, you can bake it in the oven, as I have here. Although in my hometown of London the rain has become an even more recurrent theme of late, I like to put on my raincoat and wellies and, with much persistence, get that grill going anyway.

+ Preheat the oven to 400°F.

+ Scatter the chicken pieces in a large roasting pan. Put the tomato ketchup, vinegar, soy sauce, five-spice powder and honey in a small bowl. Peel and finely chop the garlic and run your fingers down the length of the thyme sprigs to release the leaves, then add them both along with salt, pepper and a drizzle of oil. Give everything a good stir and pour it over the chicken pieces. Toss to evenly coat, then settle the chicken into a single layer and put in the oven to cook for 30 minutes.

+ Next, put the kettle on to boil for the rice.

+ Meanwhile, prepare the slaw. Remove the woody core from the cabbage and then slice the cabbage leaves up as fine as you can and put them in a large bowl. Peel and finely slice the red onion, halve, seed and finely chop the chilli and throw these in along with the raisins, mustard powder (if using) and honey. Spoon the yogurt in, squeeze in the lime juice and season to taste with salt and pepper. Mix everything together and set aside.

+ Put the rice in a medium saucepan with a little salt, pour in the now-boiled water so that it is about ¾ inch above the top of the rice, put the lid on and bring back to the boil. Then turn down the heat as low as it will go and leave to cook for as long as it says on the package.

+ Baste the chicken with the sauce.

>

Sticky Asian BBQ chicken wings with sweet corn rice & red cabbage slaw

(continued)

Once the rice is ready, drain any excess water and then put the rice back into the pan. Drain the sweet corn and add it to the rice with salt, pepper and a drizzle of oil. Stir together and then put the lid on to keep warm.

+ After the chicken has been cooking for 30 minutes, check to see that it is cooked by piercing it with a knife—it should be piping hot in the middle with no pinkness. The barbecue sauce should be a sticky coating on the chicken.

+ Divide the rice among four serving plates, arrange the chicken on top and spoon the slaw to the side. Rip the leaves from the cilantro or parsley stalks, scatter them over and serve.

Time from start to finish:
20 minutes
Serves: 4
Equipment: Kettle, large frying pan, sieve, medium saucepan with tight-fitting lid, grater

3 tbsp garam masala (easy to find in the supermarket)

1 tbsp paprika

Vegetable oil

4 skinless, boneless chicken breasts

1½ cups basmati rice

1 tsp ground turmeric or curry powder or pinch of saffron strands (optional)

1 bunch of green onions

¾-inch piece of fresh ginger

2 garlic cloves

1½ cups light cream or plain yogurt (optional; cream tastes much better but yogurt is healthier)

7 oz (¾ cup plus 2 tbsp) tomato purée

2 tsp English mustard powder

Salt and freshly ground black pepper

Fresh cilantro or parsley leaves

My take on chicken tikka masala with fluffy basmati rice

I love a good chicken tikka masala. You can try to palm me off with a dansak or a korma, but a masala will always get my taste buds going. I know just how easy it is to reach for a jar of your favorite curry sauce or tikka paste, but the thing is, I find making my own tikka masala so very rewarding; it literally takes only about 20 minutes to prepare and the bonus is you know exactly what is going onto your plate. The chicken can be replaced with butternut squash or lamb or beef (which will both need to be cooked for a bit less time) or fish (which will require even less time).

+ Put the kettle on to boil.

+ Heat a large frying pan over a medium to high heat and add the garam masala and paprika. Toast for a couple of minutes until fragrant, then transfer to a plate and set aside.

+ Drizzle some oil into the frying pan. Cut the chicken breasts into bite-size chunks and cook for 5 minutes, tossing from time to time, until brown all over.

+ Put the rice in a medium saucepan and add the turmeric (or curry powder or saffron strands), if using. Pour over enough boiled water to come about ¾ inch above the rice (roughly 2¾ cups of water, to be pedantic).

+ Cover with the lid and return to the boil. Then reduce the heat to low and leave to cook for as long as it says to on the package.

+ While the rice is cooking away, give the chicken a little toss and then trim and finely slice the green onions (both the green and the white bits), peel and grate the ginger and peel and finely chop the garlic.

>

My take on chicken tikka masala with fluffy basmati rice

(continued)

+ Add all three to the chicken along with the cream or yogurt, if using, tomato purée, the toasted spices and mustard powder. Now at this stage the sauce may not look its prettiest, but keep stirring it and once it starts looking more like the chicken tikka masala you know (and in my case love), leave it to bubble away on a low to medium heat for a few minutes to cook the chicken through.

+ Check that the rice is tender, having absorbed all the water. Fluff it up with a fork, season with salt and pepper, add a drizzle of oil, if you like, and then pop the lid on to keep the rice warm.

+ Check that the chicken is cooked—there should be no pinkness remaining. Then taste the sauce, adding more heat (with paprika) or seasoning, to your taste. If the sauce is too thick, add a little water; if it is too thin, let it bubble away a little longer to thicken.

+ Divide the rice among four plates and top with the aromatic chicken in sauce. For me, cilantro or parsley leaves ripped up on top are a must! This is my favorite Friday night feast.

Time from start to finish:
20 minutes
Serves: 4
Equipment: Baking sheet, large
frying pan, 2 medium bowls,
grater, small bowl

8 corn or wheat tortillas

Vegetable oil

4 good-size skinless, boneless chicken breasts

4 tbsp plain yogurt

4 garlic cloves

¾-inch piece of fresh ginger

3 tbsp paprika

1 tbsp garam masala (easy to find in the supermarket)

1 tsp ground coriander

1–2 tsp hot chilli powder (depending on how hot you like it)

1 lime

Salt and freshly ground black pepper

Raita

¼ cucumber

Small handful of fresh mint leaves

¾ cup plain yogurt

Salt and freshly ground black pepper

Mango salsa

1 large ripe mango or 9-oz package of prepared mango cubes

Small handful of fresh cilantro

1 lime

Salt and freshly ground black pepper

Tandoori chicken wraps with cucumber raita & mango salsa

Sandwich bars for lunch serve a very important purpose. Many times I have found myself on the go, dashing about with barely any time to sit down and eat some lunch. Making a sandwich at home is preferable, but come Thursday, inspiration for yet another sandwich is often dwindling and I am usually looking for something with a little more punch. Admittedly, cooking a dish for lunch the next day when I come home from work does prove somewhat of a challenge at the best of times, but when both my motivation and my organization are aligned, then tandoori chicken wraps are my king of on-the-go lunches.

+ Preheat the oven to 225°F.

+ Remove the tortillas from the package and place the stack on a sheet of aluminum foil. Wrap them up tightly, sit the parcel on a baking sheet and place in the oven for 10–15 minutes to warm through.

+ Put a large frying pan on a medium heat with a good drizzle of oil for the chicken. Cut the chicken into bite-size chunks and put in a medium bowl with the yogurt. Peel and grate in the garlic and then grate in the ginger also (without peeling). Then add the paprika, garam masala, ground coriander and chilli powder (as hot as you dare!), then squeeze in the lime juice and finally add salt and pepper. Mix everything together and cook, stirring from time to time, for 8–10 minutes (this will depend on the size of your chicken pieces).

+ Meanwhile, prepare the raita. Dice up the cucumber and put in a small bowl, rip up the mint leaves and then add the yogurt. Season with salt and pepper to taste, then stir, spoon into a small serving bowl and set aside.

>

Tandoori chicken wraps with cucumber raita & mango salsa

(continued)

+ Now prepare the mango salsa. If using a whole mango, slice the two cheeks off either side of the pit. Cut them in half, run the knife through the flesh close to the skin to peel it, then dice the flesh into bite-size pieces. If you are using prepared mango, cut it into small cubes. Pick and finely chop the cilantro leaves and toss these and the mango into a medium bowl. Squeeze the lime juice over, season with salt and pepper to taste, then spoon into a small serving bowl and set aside.

+ Take the tortillas from the oven, remove from the foil and place the stack on a serving plate. Check that your chicken is cooked. There should be no pinkness and it should be piping hot in the center. Spoon into a serving bowl for sharing, with the raita and mango salsa alongside.

Time from start to finish:
30 minutes
Serves: 4
Equipment: Small bowl, 2 medium bowls, baking sheet, large sauté pan or wok

Accompaniments

Small handful of fresh chives

7 oz (¾ cup plus 2 tbsp) sour cream

Small handful of fresh cilantro

1 red chilli (optional)

1 lime

7 oz cherry tomatoes

Salt and freshly ground black pepper

1 tsp sugar (optional)

2 ripe avocados

1 green onion

Fajitas

1 garlic clove

1 red onion

1 red pepper

1 orange pepper

8 corn or wheat tortillas

Spicy chicken

Olive oil

4 medium skinless, boneless chicken breasts

1 tbsp paprika

2 tsp ground cumin

1 tsp dried oregano

Salt and freshly ground black pepper

1 lime

Scrumptious spicy chicken fajitas with guacamole, salsa & sour cream

If you are like me, there have been many times when you may have reached for the package of fajitas with that sauce that you just dip in. I do know how yummy they can be, truly, but once I made my own, I never looked back. Change things up each time you make it—strips of frying beef or shrimp are a sound alternative.

+ First, prepare the accompaniments. Finely chop the chives, place in a small bowl with the sour cream and stir together.

+ Then, make the salsa and guacamole. Rip the leaves off the cilantro, roughly chop them and divide between two medium bowls. Then seed and finely chop the chilli, if using, and again, divide between the bowls. Cut the lime in half and squeeze half into each bowl also.

+ Quarter the cherry tomatoes and add to one of the bowls. Stir to combine and then season to taste with salt and pepper, also adding the sugar if you think it needs it.

+ Then, to finish the guacamole, halve the avocados, discard their pits, scoop the flesh into the other bowl and give it a little mash with a fork. Trim and finely slice the green onion (both the green and the white bits) and add also, giving everything a good mix together and season to taste.

+ Preheat the oven to 350°F.

+ Next, prepare the fajita mixture. Peel and finely chop the garlic, peel and finely slice the red onion, halve and seed the peppers and then cut each into thin strips and set aside.

+ Remove the tortillas from the package and place the stack on a sheet of aluminum foil. Wrap them up tightly, sit the parcel on a baking sheet and place in the oven for 10–15 minutes to warm through.

>

Scrumptious spicy chicken fajitas with guacamole, salsa & sour cream

(continued)

+ Meanwhile, cook the chicken. Put a good drizzle of oil in a large sauté pan or wok over a high heat. While the oil heats up, cut the chicken into short, thin strips and then carefully add them to the hot oil. Cook for 2–3 minutes, stirring from time to time, until they start turning golden brown.

+ Add the paprika, cumin and oregano and season well with salt and pepper. Halve the lime and squeeze in the juice and then add the reserved garlic, red onion and peppers.

+ Reduce the heat to medium and keep everything cooking for another 6–8 minutes or until the chicken is piping hot and cooked through with no pinkness and the peppers are just beginning to soften, then remove from the heat.

+ Spoon the accompaniments into serving bowls. Remove the tortillas from the oven, carefully unwrap and stack on a serving plate.

+ Spoon the cooked chicken mixture into a serving bowl. My family likes this served with everything in the middle of the table. Then it is a big free-for-all as everyone dives in!

Time from start to finish:
35 minutes
Serves: 4
Equipment: Large sauté pan,
scissors, kettle, large saucepan
with lid, colander

Vegetable oil

4 strips of bacon

4 skinless, boneless chicken breasts or
8 skinless, boneless chicken thighs

Salt and freshly ground black pepper

1 bunch of green onions

5 oz cremini or black poplar
mushrooms

2 garlic cloves

2 sprigs of fresh rosemary

Two 14-oz cans of chopped tomatoes

A good glug (about ½ cup) of
Madeira (or red or white wine or
chicken stock)

1 tbsp harissa paste (you can get it
from most supermarkets) or 3 tbsp
tomato purée

Pinch of dried oregano

1 dried bay leaf

11 oz of your favorite pasta (I love to
use penne or rigatoni)

1–2 tsp sugar (optional)

Pat of butter (optional)

Small handful of fresh basil or parsley
leaves (optional)

Chicken cacciatore with harissa, bacon & rosemary

Recently, I have become a bit of a chicken thigh person, finding the meat moister and more succulent than the ubiquitous chicken breast. The addition of harissa, the spicy, tomato-y Moroccan paste, adds a subtle kick to this "hunter-style" Italian dish, but for those not in love with an extra bit of spice, then tomato purée works beautifully too.

+ Put a drizzle of oil into a large sauté pan on a high heat. Use scissors to snip the bacon into bite-size pieces. Add them to the pan once hot and fry for a couple of minutes, stirring every so often, until they are browned.

+ While the bacon cooks, season the chicken pieces well with salt and pepper.

+ Remove the bacon from the pan, leaving the fat behind, and set aside to drain on paper towels. Put the chicken in, top side down, reduce the heat to medium and leave to cook for about 4 minutes.

+ Meanwhile, trim and finely slice the green onions (both the green and the white bits) and mushrooms and peel and finely chop the garlic. Run your fingers down the length of the rosemary stalks to release their leaves and finely chop them too. Set everything aside.

+ The chicken pieces should now be golden brown underneath, so flip them over and leave to cook on the other side for about 3 minutes.

+ Once the chicken is golden brown, turn down the heat to low and add the prepared mushrooms, garlic and rosemary, along with the tomatoes, Madeira (or red or white wine or stock), harissa paste or tomato purée and oregano, and crumble in the bay leaf.

+ Give it a good stir and then leave to bubble away for 15–20 minutes, stirring from time to time so that it does not stick to the bottom.

>

Chicken cacciatore with harissa, bacon & rosemary

(continued)

+ When the chicken dish is about halfway through cooking, add the reserved cooked bacon and green onions, then put the kettle on. Use the boiled water to cook the pasta in a large saucepan according to the package's instructions. Once it is cooked, drain the pasta and then return it to the pan with the lid on to keep warm if necessary.

+ Check to see if the chicken is cooked—if the juices run clear, it is ready. Taste the sauce, adding a little sugar and/or a pat of butter if the sauce is still a bit acidic from the tomatoes. Add a drizzle of water if the sauce is too thick and let it bubble away for a bit longer if too thin.

+ Divide the pasta among four plates, top with a piece of chicken breast or two thighs, spoon some sauce over and scatter with some ripped-up basil or parsley leaves, if using.

Time from start to finish:
35 minutes
Serves: 4
Equipment: Large roasting pan,
peeler, large sauté pan or
casserole dish with tight–fitting
lid, large plate

1½ lbs baby or new potatoes

3 large carrots

Salt and freshly ground black pepper

Vegetable oil

1 tbsp fennel seeds

8 chicken thighs, skin on and bone in

12 cocktail sausages or 4 regular sausages

2 sprigs of fresh rosemary

A few sprigs of fresh sage

2 garlic cloves

1 bunch of green onions

2 Granny Smith apples

4 tsp all-purpose flour

2 cups cider (or chicken stock)

Chicken, apple & cider casserole with fennel seed roasted veg

I made this dish with regular sausages, but once the dish was ready, each sausage had shot right out of its jacket. Not a problem for most—in fact they are just the ticket to provide some cheap humor at the dinner table—but this problem can easily be solved by carefully removing the skins from the sausages before adding them to the casserole with the chicken.

+ Preheat the oven to 425°F.

+ Slice the potatoes into very thin slices and scatter them into a large roasting pan. Peel and slice the carrots into ⅜-inch pieces and scatter them over. Season everything well with salt and pepper and drizzle with oil. Scatter the fennel seeds over, toss gently together and lay everything out in as even a layer as possible. Place in the oven to roast for 30 minutes.

+ Next put some oil in a large sauté pan or casserole dish over a high heat. While this heats up, season the chicken with a good amount of salt and pepper and then put half of the chicken in the pan, skin side down. Nestle half of the sausages around the chicken and cook for 4 minutes. Don't move the chicken but turn the sausages every so often to give them a nice golden color all over.

+ Meanwhile, run your fingers down the length of the rosemary sprigs to release the leaves, pick the sage leaves and then set them aside.

+ Once the chicken skin is crisp and golden brown, flip the pieces over and let the "meaty" side cook for 1 minute. Then remove the chicken and sausages from the pan and place on a large plate. Repeat with the remaining chicken and sausages.

+ Peel and finely slice the garlic and then trim and chop the green onions (both the green and the white bits) into ⅜-inch pieces. Quarter the apples,

>

Chicken, apple & cider casserole with fennel seed roasted veg

(continued)

remove their cores and then cut each piece in half again. Set them aside with the herbs.

+ Check on the potatoes and carrots, giving them a gentle toss before returning to the oven.

+ Once all of the chicken thighs and the sausages are seared and on the plate, remove the pan from the heat. Tilt the pan a little to one side so that the oil can gather in a pool. Add the flour to the oil and mix together to make a paste. Then, setting the pan back down, gradually add the cider (or chicken stock), stirring all the time so that there are no lumps, and then put the pan back on a high heat. Bring to the boil and then let it bubble away for a couple of minutes.

+ Once the sauce is thickened slightly, stir in the herbs, garlic and apples, season with salt and pepper and then set the chicken and sausages in the sauce. Everything won't be completely immersed, but nestle them in as best you can. Turn the heat down to medium, cover with the lid and allow the dish to bubble away gently for 15 minutes. Then 5 minutes before the chicken is ready, add the green onions.

+ Once the chicken and sausages are cooked (they will be piping hot in the middle with no pink meat), remove them from the heat. The potatoes and carrots should be tender when pierced with a knife and with golden tinges. Remove them from the oven and serve with the casserole.

Time from start to finish:
15 minutes
Serves: 4
Equipment: Medium frying pan, small saucepan, grater, medium sauté pan or wok, plate

Vegetable oil

4 duck breasts

Salt and freshly ground black pepper

1 tbsp Chinese five-spice powder

Sauce

½ cup Shiraz red wine (or chicken stock or water)

4 tbsp cherry jam (plum will work fine too)

3 tbsp soy sauce

¾-inch piece of fresh ginger

Salt and freshly ground black pepper

Noodles

1 bunch of green onions

1 garlic clove

Sesame oil

5 oz fine asparagus, woody ends trimmed off

2 tbsp sesame seeds

2 tbsp soy sauce

11 oz straight-to-wok noodles

Salt and freshly ground black pepper

Fresh cilantro leaves (optional)

Five-spice roasted duck breasts with cherry & Shiraz sauce & sesame noodles

Duck is a wonderful meat to cook. I am a great fan of its meaty-flavored flesh and a lover of its perfectly crisped-up skin. There will be loads of fat left in the pan from cooking the duck. I pour the fat into a jar and save it in the fridge for when I cook my roast potatoes on Sunday.

+ Put a little drizzle of oil in a medium frying pan and get it nice and hot. While this heats up, use a sharp knife to make 3–4 slashes in the skin of the duck (but not down to the flesh). This will help the skin to crisp up. Season the breasts well with salt and pepper and then rub the five-spice powder all over. Place them skin side down in the hot pan and leave them to cook on a medium heat for about 5 minutes.

+ As the duck cooks, trim and halve the green onions for the noodles, then slice them lengthwise into thin strips. Peel and finely chop the garlic and set both aside.

+ Next make the sauce. Put the Shiraz red wine (or stock or water), jam and soy sauce into a small saucepan over a really low heat and then peel and grate in the ginger. Give it a good stir and leave to bubble away gently on a medium heat for 8 minutes or so.

+ When the duck skin is crisp, flip the breasts over, turn the heat down quite low and leave to cook for a further 8 minutes.

+ Next prepare the noodles. Add a good glug of sesame oil to a medium sauté pan or wok and get it nice and hot. Add the prepared green onions and garlic and the asparagus and cook for 2–3 minutes, tossing occasionally, until slightly wilted. Then add the sesame seeds, soy sauce and noodles and cook the noodles for as long as it says to on the package (it should only be a few minutes), again tossing from time to time.

>

Five-spice roasted duck breasts with cherry & Shiraz sauce & sesame noodles

(continued)

+ Check the duck breasts. When cooked they should be piping hot in the middle. I test mine by inserting a skewer into the center and leaving it for a moment, then pulling it out and carefully testing the temperature on my hand.

+ Remove the cooked duck breasts to a plate, then cover loosely with aluminum foil to rest for a few minutes. This will make the flesh much more juicy.

+ By now, the sauce should be thickened and syrupy. Season with salt and pepper to taste.

+ Finally, once the noodles are cooked, season them to taste with salt and pepper and then divide them among four plates and top each with a duck breast. Drizzle the sauce over, rip over some cilantro leaves, it you fancy, and serve.

Beef, lamb + pork mains

Observe the masses and do the opposite.
Walt Disney

It has only been in recent years that I have really got into beef, lamb and pork. And my goodness, have I got into them. I suppose before I became a chef, I was not really sure what to do with these three majestic meats. But then I started buying different cuts and types and began experimenting, messing around with flavors and colors and textures. I believe that a lot of the time, unless you can spend a hefty sum on meat (or have the luxury of a butcher right on your doorstep), it does not taste so good. However, with a little bit of help from various spice rack staples, handsome herbs and other easy ingredients, these familiar meats can be turned into something really special for quick and easy meals.

Time from start to finish:
35 minutes
Serves: **4**
Equipment: **Large baking tray, large bowl, large frying pan, plate, baking tray**

Potato wedges

4 large baking potatoes

8 garlic cloves

Olive oil

Salt and freshly ground black pepper

Burgers

½ bunch of green onions

1 garlic clove

1 lb lean ground beef

2 oz (¼ cup) dried plain breadcrumbs

Big dollop (about 1 tbsp) of yellow mustard

A couple of squeezes (about 1 tbsp) of tomato ketchup

A few shakes of Worcestershire sauce

1 medium egg

2 sprigs of fresh thyme

Salt and freshly ground black pepper

Olive oil

To serve

1 large tomato

4 oz Cheddar or blue cheese

1 small red onion

4 burger buns (I like mine with a sesame seed top)

A little butter (optional)

A few dollops of yellow mustard

1 bag of wild arugula

Extra virgin olive oil

Balsamic vinegar

Ketchup or HP sauce (optional)

Good old-fashioned burger with arugula, red onions (plus all the trimmings) & garlicky potato wedges

I tested these over and over again to get the flavors just right. A squeeze of this there and a dollop of that here and I think I have got it just right.

+ Preheat the oven to 425°F.

+ Cut each potato in half lengthwise and then cut each piece into four or five long wedges. Peel the garlic and slam it with the side of a knife to slightly crush. Toss both onto a large baking tray, drizzle a good amount of oil over and season with salt and pepper. Toss everything together and then even out into a single layer. Roast in the oven for 30 minutes.

+ Meanwhile, trim and really finely slice the green onions (both the green and white bits), peel and finely chop the garlic and add both to a large bowl. Add the ground beef, breadcrumbs, yellow mustard, tomato ketchup and Worcestershire sauce and crack in the egg.

+ Slide your thumb and forefinger down the thyme sprigs to remove the leaves in one go and add those to the bowl with a good amount of salt and pepper.

+ Before you get your hands into the mixture, put a good drizzle of oil in a large frying pan on a high heat. Then back to the mixture and press it together with your hands until everything is well combined. Divide into four equal-size pieces, shape each into a 1-inch-thick patty and place all on a plate.

+ Carefully add the burgers to the pan, reduce the heat to medium and leave to fry on the first side for 5–6 minutes.

+ As the burgers cook, slice up the tomato and cheese (or crumble the blue cheese, if using). Peel and finely slice the onion.

>

Good old-fashioned burger with arugula, red onions (plus all the trimmings) & garlicky potato wedges

(continued)

+ Give the potatoes a good toss and flip the burgers over when ready. The burgers will need another 5–8 minutes, depending on how well you like them cooked.

+ Split the burger buns open, arrange on a baking tray and put them into the oven for a few minutes to crisp up.

+ Remove the buns from the oven, buttering them if you fancy. Check that your burgers are cooked as you like them and place each one on a burger bun base. Layer up the tomato, cheese, onion and mustard whichever way you like and then finish with the burger bun top.

+ Serve with the potato wedges from the oven and a handful of arugula drizzled with some olive oil and balsamic vinegar. I just have to serve these with tomato ketchup or HP sauce.

Time from start to finish:
40 minutes
Serves: **4**
Equipment: **Baking tray, 2 medium bowls, casserole dish or large pan, medium frying pan**

Dumplings

1 cup self-rising flour

3 oz (⅓ cup) shredded beef or vegetable suet

Small handful of fresh thyme sprigs

1 medium egg

¼ cup water

Stew

Vegetable oil

Pat of butter

5 oz bacon (the oak-smoked one is great, but regular is fine too), cut into cubes

1 bunch of green onions

2 garlic cloves

5 fresh sage leaves

1 lb prepared butternut squash and sweet potato mix

1 oz sundried tomatoes

4 tbsp all-purpose flour

2 oz dried porcini mushrooms

2 tbsp plum or cherry jam (optional)

1 bay leaf

A few shakes of Worcestershire sauce

2 cups beef stock

1 cup port (or if you don't want to use alcohol, just make this amount up with stock)

1 lb beef rump steak

1 tbsp English mustard powder

Salt and freshly ground black pepper

Fresh flat leaf parsley (optional)

Rich rump steak "sort-of-stew" with port, porcini & herby dumplings

I wanted to include a stew in this book, but with the word "fast" in the title, I had really set myself a challenge. I remember those days at school, all the children huddled around the table, chattering between mouthfuls of pillowy herbed dumplings moistened slightly with the gravy of the stew. That meat was perhaps not A1, but the feeling of something warm and comforting inside made up for it. This stew is made in parts and then assembled at the end. You could make it with stewing beef over a long period of time, but more liquid would need to be added to compensate for the longer cooking. And, of course, sirloin can be substituted for rump, which is higher in fat, but for me has a little more flavor.

+ Preheat the oven to 400°F. Oil a baking tray and set aside.

+ First make the dumplings. Put the self-rising flour and suet into a medium bowl and slide your fingers down the thyme sprigs to add the leaves. Give a quick mix with a spoon and add the egg with the water and mix to combine to give a smooth dough.

+ At this stage I like to get my hands into the bowl and form the mixture into 12 even-size round dumplings. Place them spaced apart on the baking tray as you go and then bake in the oven for 15–20 minutes.

+ My speedy shortcut for this stew is to get the sauce cooking first before the meat. Heat a drizzle of oil and pat of butter in a casserole dish or large pan on a high heat. Add the bacon and cook for 2–3 minutes, stirring now and again, until crisp and golden.

>

Rich rump steak "sort—of—stew" with port, porcini & herby dumplings

(continued)

+ Meanwhile, finely slice up the green onions (the green and white bits), peel and roughly chop the garlic and roughly chop the sage and add to the cooked bacon. Cut the butternut squash and sweet potato pieces in half if large and then add to the pan and sweat for 2–3 minutes.

+ Roughly chop the sundried tomatoes and add to the pan along with 3 tablespoons of the flour, the dried porcini mushrooms, jam to sweeten (if using), bay leaf and Worcestershire sauce. Stir together before adding the beef stock and port (if using). Turn up the heat and let it boil away to reduce for about 10 minutes or so until thickened.

+ While this is bubbling away, put a medium frying pan on a low heat with a good drizzle of oil. While the oil is heating up, trim the rump steak of excess fat, cut into big bite-size chunks and put in a medium bowl. Add the remaining tablespoon of flour, the mustard powder and a good amount of salt and pepper and then toss everything together so the meat is well coated.

+ Turn the heat up to high under the frying pan and carefully add about half of the meat. Brown it well all over for 2–3 minutes before transferring to a plate and repeating with the next batch. Doing it in small batches like this means the meat will brown nicely rather than stew in its juices, which adds to the flavor.

+ Season the sauce with salt and pepper to taste and carefully return the meat and any juices to the casserole. Spoon a little of the sauce into the meat-searing pan and simmer on a low heat for a minute or two, scraping any sticky bits from the bottom. Return this to the stew for extra flavor, reduce the heat and leave to simmer away very gently for about another 10 minutes until the meat and vegetables are tender and the sauce thickened and rich.

+ Remove the dumplings from the oven. They should be crusty and golden on the outside and cooked through.

+ Then, to serve, I either take the stew straight to the table in the casserole dish with the dumplings nestled on top or divide it among four plates, arranging a few dumplings on each one. Either way, roughly chop the parsley (if using) and scatter over to serve.

Rosemary roast cottage pie with a crispy rosti topping

Prep time: **25 minutes**
Time baking in the oven:
25 minutes
Serves: **4**
Equipment: **Large pan, peeler, sieve set over a small bowl, kettle, medium saucepan, grater, small pan (or bowl and microwave), 8-inch square baking dish at least 2 inches deep (about 2 quarts), medium bowl**

Not a pint-sized list of ingredients, I agree, but family demands for inclusion of a cottage pie had to be met. The crispy rosti topping adds some welcome crunch to this classic British dish.

Pie filling

Vegetable oil
2 sprigs of fresh rosemary
4 fresh sage leaves
1½ lbs ground lamb
3 carrots
1 garlic clove
1 green onion
14-oz can of chopped tomatoes
2 tbsp all-purpose flour
1½ cups beef stock (or a good red wine or Madeira)
4 oz (½ cup) tomato purée
2 tbsp Worcestershire sauce
1 handful (about 1 oz) of dried porcini mushrooms (optional)
1 tsp sugar
Salt and freshly ground black pepper
4 oz frozen peas

Rosti

1 medium potato
1 medium sweet potato
2 oz Cheddar cheese (optional)
2 tbsp butter
Whole nutmeg (optional)

Salad

4 tbsp extra virgin olive oil
2 tbsp balsamic vinegar
1 tsp Dijon mustard
Salt and freshly ground black pepper
2 bags of wild arugula or mixed leaves

+ Preheat the oven to 400°F.

+ Place a large pan, with a good drizzle of oil, on a high heat for the cottage pie filling. Run your fingers down the length of the rosemary to release the leaves and then roughly chop them along with the sage. Add to the pan with the lamb and leave to cook for 4–5 minutes or until the meat is browned all over, stirring occasionally.

+ While that is cooking away, peel the carrots and cut them into small dice and peel and finely chop the garlic. Stir them into the browned meat and cook for a further minute or two. Finely chop the green onion (both the green and white bits) and set aside.

+ Meanwhile, drain the can of tomatoes through a sieve set over a small bowl to catch the juice. Then stir the flour into the meat mixture really well before adding the tomatoes from the sieve. (You are not using the juice in this recipe but it can be frozen for later use in a soup or stew for example.)

+ Add the stock (or red wine or Madeira), tomato purée, Worcestershire sauce and dried porcini mushrooms (if using) and stir a couple of times before leaving it to bubble away for about 15 minutes.

+ In the meantime, prepare the rosti topping. Put the kettle on. Peel the potatoes, cut the white one in half (leaving the sweet potato whole) and place them into a medium saucepan with a little salt. Cover them with the boiled water and return to the boil on a high heat before reducing to simmer for about 5 minutes.

+ While they are cooking, you can roughly grate the cheese (if using) and set it aside for the topping. Melt the butter for the rosti in a small pan (or bowl in the microwave) and set aside also.

>

Rosemary roast cottage pie with a crispy rosti topping

(continued)

+ When the potatoes have been cooking for about 5 minutes, drain them really well and set them aside for a few minutes or until cool enough to handle.

+ Roughly grate the potatoes, toss them together gently on a board and season them really well with salt and pepper.

+ Remove the meat mixture from the heat, add the green onion and season to taste with salt and pepper. I also like to add a little sugar to soften the sharpness of the tomatoes. Stir the frozen peas in and put the whole thing in the baking dish.

+ Scatter the potato mixture over the pie, fluffing it up a bit with a fork, then gently brush the melted butter over the top. Grate over some nutmeg, if using, and bake in the oven for 25 minutes.

+ Scatter the cheese over 5 minutes before the end of the cooking time. Then mix the oil, balsamic vinegar, Dijon mustard and some salt and pepper together in a medium bowl. Toss the arugula or mixed leaves through to dress.

+ Once cooked, the potato should be tender all the way through, crispy on top and just catching color. Remove the cottage pie from the oven and serve straight to the table with the bowl of dressed leaves.

Time from start to finish:
30 minutes
Serves: **4**
Equipment: Kettle, large sauté pan (preferably not nonstick), scissors, medium saucepan with tight-fitting lid, plate

Sunflower oil

2 sirloin steaks (about 8 oz each)

Salt and freshly ground black pepper

2 cups Thai jasmine rice

1 red pepper

1 eggplant

2 garlic cloves

1¾-inch piece of fresh ginger

6 tbsp Thai red curry paste

Two 14-oz cans of coconut milk

3 tbsp fish sauce

1 bunch of green onions

1 handful of seedless red grapes (about 2 oz) (optional)

Small handful of fresh basil leaves

Thai red beef curry with jasmine rice

Last year the family went to Thailand as a Christmas treat. We stayed in the most beautiful hotel with views over the vibrant aquamarine sea. Every day I would order the same thing for dinner: the red beef curry. The heat of the ginger, the creaminess of the coconut milk and the sweetness of the red grapes made for a multilayered taste extravaganza that I just had to re-create at home. The beef can be replaced by chicken or even butternut squash for a simple variation.

+ Put the kettle on to boil and put a large sauté pan on a medium to high heat with a drizzle of oil in.

+ Meanwhile, cut the fat off the sides of the steaks (I find the easiest way to do this is with scissors). Season the steaks really well with a good amount of salt and pepper and then lower them into the hot fat and leave to cook for about 3 minutes.

+ Meanwhile, put the rice in a medium saucepan. Pour over enough boiled water to come about ¾ inch above the rice (roughly 2 cups of water, to be pedantic). Cover with the lid and return to the boil. Then reduce the heat to low and leave to cook for as long as it says to on the package.

+ Next halve and seed the pepper, then cut it into big bite-size chunks and set aside.

+ Flip the steaks over to the other side and cook for another 3 minutes.

+ Continue to prepare the vegetables. Trim and cut the eggplant into big bite-size pieces, peel and finely chop the garlic and peel and slice the ginger into sticks.

+ Remove the steaks from the pan (leaving the pan on the heat) and leave to rest on a plate, covered with aluminum foil.

>

Thai red beef curry with jasmine rice

(continued)

+ Pour 1 tablespoon of water into the pan and scrape up any tasty bits left from the steak. Stir in the curry paste and allow to cook for 30 seconds. Then add the red pepper, eggplant, garlic and ginger. Stir well together to combine and pour in the coconut milk and fish sauce. Turn up the heat, bring to the boil and then reduce the heat a little and leave it to bubble away gently for 8 minutes.

+ Check that the rice is now tender and, if so, remove from the heat, fluff up with a fork and cover with the lid to keep warm.

+ Next slice up the green onions (the green and white bits) and halve the grapes (if using) and set them aside.

+ Slice up the rested beef into very thin slivers. Then add them to the curry along with the resting juices, green onions and grapes (if using). Season to taste with salt and pepper and a little more fish sauce, if desired, and then cook for another minute or so.

+ Divide the rice among four plates and top with the curry. Sprinkle over the basil and serve.

Prep time: **30 minutes**
Time baking in the oven:
20 minutes
Serves: **6**
Equipment: **Kettle, 10-inch square baking dish about 2½ inches deep (2½ quarts), baking tray, small saucepan with lid, large frying pan, 2 medium bowls, colander, grater, mug or small bowl**

3 medium potatoes

Pinch of salt

Vegetable oil

1¼ lbs ground lamb (or beef)

1 bunch of green onions

2 garlic cloves

2 tbsp all-purpose flour

14-oz can of chopped tomatoes (the ones with the herbs are nice but not essential)

1 glass (about 1 cup) of a good red wine (or Marsala or beef or chicken stock)

6 tbsp Worcestershire sauce

4 tbsp tomato purée

1 tbsp ground cumin

3 tsp ground cinnamon

3 tsp dried oregano

2 sprigs of fresh thyme

Salt and freshly ground black pepper

1 large eggplant

Olive oil

Small handful of fresh mint

White sauce

4 oz Parmesan cheese

9-oz tub of ricotta cheese

2 medium egg yolks

A pinch of freshly grated nutmeg

Salt and freshly ground black pepper

Salad

6 tbsp extra virgin olive oil

3 tbsp red wine vinegar

Salt and freshly ground black pepper

1 bag of watercress leaves

The mighty moussaka

I squeezed this dish into the book as it is faster than most moussakas. I know it may not be the most pure of moussaka recipes, but for my family it is one that both satisfies the tummy and pleases the palate. All the sauce ingredients go straight in the pan and I have also come up with a simple "white sauce," which can be made in a matter of seconds and is rich and creamy and incredibly flavorsome.

+ Preheat the oven to 425°F and put the kettle on to boil for the potatoes. Sit the baking dish on a baking tray and set aside.

+ Wash the potatoes well and then slice them up into ¼-inch-thick rounds. Place in a small saucepan with a pinch of salt and pour the now-boiled water over. Put on a high heat with the lid on to bring the water back to the boil quickly.

+ Meanwhile, put a drizzle of oil in a large frying pan over a really high heat. Fry half of the lamb (or beef) for a few minutes, stirring regularly, until it all gets nice and colored. Put it in a medium bowl while you brown the remaining meat.

+ Once the potato pan is boiling away, remove the lid and leave to cook for about 8 minutes.

+ Next, slice up the green onions (both the green and white bits) and peel and slice the garlic.

+ Return all the meat to the pan and stir in the flour. Then add the green onions, garlic, tomatoes, red wine (or Marsala or beef or chicken stock), Worcestershire sauce, tomato purée, cumin, cinnamon and oregano. Run your fingers down the length of the thyme sprigs to release their leaves and add them with some salt and pepper. Stir well and cook on a low heat for 5 minutes. Give it a stir from time to time so it does not stick on the bottom.

>

The mighty moussaka

(continued)

+ Check that the potatoes are just tender (but not fully cooked), then drain them in a colander, season with salt and pepper and set them aside for a moment.

+ Next make the white sauce. Finely grate the Parmesan, reserve a big handful for later and put the remainder into a medium bowl. Add the ricotta, egg yolks, nutmeg and salt and pepper. Stir well and set aside.

+ Trim and slice the eggplant into very thin rounds. Remove the now-cooked meat filling from the heat.

+ Now for the assembly. Arrange half of the eggplant slices in a layer in the bottom of the baking dish, drizzle with some oil and season with salt and pepper. Spread half of the meat on top, followed by a layer of half of the potatoes. Repeat these three layers again and then dot the white sauce over the top before spreading it evenly to cover. Scatter the reserved Parmesan over and bake for 20 minutes or until golden brown.

+ Five minutes before the moussaka is ready, whisk up the oil, vinegar and some salt and pepper for the dressing in a mug or small bowl. Put the watercress into a large salad bowl, drizzle the dressing over and toss to coat.

+ When the moussaka is ready, remove from the oven, rip over the mint leaves and serve with the dressed salad.

20 minutes
Serves: **4**
Equipment: **Kettle, large frying
pan, 2 large plates, medium
bowl, small saucepan**

Couscous

1½ cups couscous

7 oz good feta cheese

Salt and freshly ground black pepper

A drizzle of extra virgin olive oil

Lamb

Vegetable oil

Large handful of fresh thyme sprigs

Salt and freshly ground black pepper

8 lamb chops or cutlets

1 bunch of green onions

2 oz flaked almonds

Glaze

2 tbsp butter

2 tbsp maple syrup

1 tbsp balsamic vinegar

To serve

Small handful of fresh mint

A handful of pomegranate seeds
(optional)

Maple and balsamic-glazed lamb chops with mint, toasted almonds & feta couscous

Not a reinvention of the wheel with these flavor combos,
but a simple, seductive supper nonetheless. I do away
with knives and forks for these little lamb chops and
with messy fingers gnaw off the meat, right down to
the bone.

+ Put the kettle on to boil for the couscous.

+ Meanwhile, put a large frying pan on a medium heat with a good glug
of vegetable oil. Run your fingers down the thyme sprigs to release their
leaves and sprinkle them all over a large plate. Add a little salt and
pepper and then press the lamb chops or cutlets into the mix, turning
them over to coat the other side also. This will give a lovely crust when
cooked. Fry them in the pan for 3–4 minutes on the first side or until they
are golden brown.

+ Put the couscous in a medium bowl, pour the boiled water over to come
just a little over the top of the grains, cover with plastic wrap and set
aside for 8 minutes.

+ Meanwhile, trim and slice the green onions (both the green and white
bits) and set aside.

+ For the glaze, put the butter, maple syrup and balsamic vinegar into a
small saucepan over a high heat. Bring to the boil and then reduce to
simmer, leaving it to bubble away for about 3 minutes, stirring from time
to time.

+ Flip the lamb chops over and leave to cook for a further 3–4 minutes,
depending on how well done you like them.

>

Maple and balsamic-glazed lamb chops with mint, toasted almonds & feta couscous

(continued)

+ Check that the couscous grains have absorbed all the water and are tender and them fluff them up with a fork. Crumble the feta cheese in, season with salt and pepper and add a good drizzle of oil. Stir together and re-cover to keep warm.

+ The glaze should be thickened and syrupy (a little bit thinner than corn syrup), so remove from the heat and keep warm.

+ Cut into the center of one of the lamb chops or cutlets to check that it is cooked to your liking. When ready, remove them onto a large plate to rest for a few minutes, covered with aluminum foil (this will make them much more tender and juicy).

+ Add the green onions and flaked almonds to the frying pan and cook on a medium heat for 1–2 minutes, stirring them a bit every now and then. Remove from the heat when the onions are wilted and the almonds golden.

+ Divide the couscous among four serving plates. Sit the rested lamb chops on top and drizzle the glaze (and any resting juices) over. Scatter over the onion and almond mix and tear the mint leaves over. If using, top with the pomegranate seeds and serve.

Time from start to finish:
25 minutes
Serves: **4**
Equipment: **Medium saucepan with tight-fitting lid, sieve**

Vegetable oil

5 cardamom pods

2 tsp garam masala (easy to find in the supermarket)

2 tsp ground turmeric

1 tsp ground cumin

1 tsp hot or medium chilli powder (or more if you want a bit of extra heat)

1 bunch of green onions

1 lb lamb top sirloin steaks

2 cups basmati rice

12-oz can of coconut milk

½ cup water

4 oz sundried tomatoes

Small handful of fresh cilantro or mint

2 oz raisins

Salt and freshly ground black pepper

Pat of butter (optional)

1 oz toasted flaked almonds (they come ready toasted from the supermarket)

Lozza's lamb biryani

My close friends call me Lozza, so I could not resist using my nickname for alliteration in the name of this recipe! This also works really well with chicken, beef or shrimp instead of the lamb. Now, it is not strictly a traditional recipe, but it is packed full of wonderful flavors and is a pretty good imitation. I believe that traditionally this Moghul dish is flavored with saffron, which I have left out, but feel free to add a stamen or two to the rice if you fancy it.

+ Put a drizzle of oil in a medium saucepan on a low heat. Slam the cardamom pods open with the side of a knife and add to the pan with the garam masala, turmeric, cumin and chilli powder and cook for 3–4 minutes, stirring occasionally.

+ While this cooks, trim and finely slice the green onions (both the green and the white bits) and then chop the lamb up into bite-size cubes. Turn the pan heat up to high, add a little more oil and add the green onions and lamb. Brown the meat all over for 2–3 minutes, stirring often so nothing sticks to the bottom.

+ Then add the rice to the pan with the coconut milk and the water.

+ Cover with a tight-fitting lid, bring to the boil and then turn it down to a very gentle simmer and leave to cook away for as long as it says to on the rice package (usually 10–12 minutes). Don't be tempted to stir the rice.

+ Meanwhile, roughly chop up the sundried tomatoes and the cilantro or mint and set aside.

+ Once the rice is cooked, stir in the sundried tomatoes, half the cilantro or mint and the raisins. Let them heat through for a moment or two.

+ Taste the rice, adding any salt and pepper if it needs it and even a pat of butter to make it extra creamy, if you like. Then serve with a scattering of the remaining chopped herbs over the top along with the toasted flaked almonds, if using.

Prep time: **10 minutes**
Time baking in the oven: **4 hours**
Serves: **4**
Equipment: **Casserole dish (big enough to fit the lamb) with lid, roasting pan**

½ leg of lamb (the thick fillet end), with bone in (about 2¼ lbs)

Salt and freshly ground black pepper

2 red onions

8 garlic cloves

4 sprigs of fresh rosemary

4 fresh sage leaves

2 bay leaves

1½ cups white wine (any wine will do)

A couple of dabs of honey

1¼ lbs roasting potatoes

Olive oil

11 oz frozen peas

Slow-roast, fast-prep leg of lamb with Aussie Chardonnay, rosemary, sage & bay

Now, this is a slow-cook but very fast-prep dish, so I thought I would add it to the book. I made this at home one Sunday. I literally just lobbed all the ingredients in the pot and then left it to cook for ages. I seriously was not expecting anything amazing; just, I thought, a bit of lamb for dinner. But when it was cooked, I tasted a little while it was still on the kitchen counter and I almost ate the whole darn lot and did that little dance people sometimes do when something tastes really good. When I took it to the kitchen table to my hungry family, basically half eaten, they were, to say the least, not amused. I ended up slinging some chops on the grill to make up for it. (Methinks I am perhaps revealing too much here!) I am not ashamed to admit I love a good Aussie Chard and the powerful flavors work well in this dish. Having said that, any white wine will be great to cook with too.

+ Remove the lamb from the fridge 30 minutes before cooking (to bring it to room temperature), if you have time. Preheat the oven to 300°F, and make sure the racks are set to fit the casserole dish and roasting pan.

+ Place the lamb in the casserole dish and season it really well with salt and pepper. Cut the onions into quarters, keeping the roots intact, peel off the skin and throw the onions in along with the (unpeeled) garlic cloves, rosemary sprigs, sage and bay leaves. Pour in the white wine

>

Slow-roast, fast-prep leg of lamb with Aussie Chardonnay, rosemary, sage & bay

(continued)

and drizzle the honey over. Put the lid on and place the whole thing in the oven, leaving it for about 4 hours. Set a timer for 2 hours 30 minutes as that's when you need to add the potatoes.

+ While I am still in the kitchen, I peel the potatoes and cut them into small roastie sizes. Then I toss them in a roasting pan with a good drizzle of oil and leave them to sit. (They won't go brown with the oil on.)

+ When the meat has been cooking for 2½ hours, season the potatoes with salt and pepper, drizzle a bit more oil on them if they have sucked it all up and place them in the oven. Give them a toss about every so often.

+ Finally, 10 minutes before the meat is ready, throw the peas into the lamb cooking juices.

+ Once everything is cooked, remove the pan from the oven. The meat should fall off the bone easily and the potatoes should be crisp and golden. There is no need to rest the meat after this long cooking time, so simply dish up and serve.

Pork balls

6 large herby sausages

3 oz dried plain breadcrumbs

1 medium egg

Salt and freshly ground black pepper

Vegetable oil

Sweet and sour sauce

1 garlic clove

1 red pepper

15-oz can of pineapple chunks in syrup

10 squeezes of tomato ketchup (about ⅓ cup)

5 tbsp balsamic vinegar (about ⅓ cup)

2–3 dabs of honey

1 lime

Crunchy peanut rice

2¾ cups instant long-grain rice

3 oz roasted, salted peanuts

½ bunch of green onions

Pat of butter

Salt and freshly ground black pepper

Sweet & sour pork balls with crunchy peanut rice

These pork balls are delicious, but when you are not feeling as if you want to make them from scratch, the markets sell some premade meatballs that you can also use with this sauce. But I like to have the choice of using really scrumptious sausage meat for maximum flavor impact!

+ Snip the skin off the sausages with scissors and then use your hands to peel it off and discard. Put the sausage meat in a large bowl with the breadcrumbs, then crack the egg in, season with salt and pepper and mix everything together well.

+ Drizzle some oil into a large sauté pan and place on a medium heat.

+ Roll the sausage mix into 20 equal-size balls, about 1¼ inches in diameter. Add them to the heated pan and cook for about 8 minutes, turning them every so often so they brown nicely all over.

+ Put the kettle on to boil for the rice.

+ At this point I like to get ahead with some prep for the sauce. Peel and finely chop the garlic and halve and seed the red pepper, then finely slice it and set aside for a minute.

+ Put the rice in a saucepan and, when the kettle has boiled, add enough hot water so that it comes about ¾ inch above the top of the rice. Then pop the lid on and cook for as long as it says to on the package.

+ Once the meatballs have browned, add the prepared garlic and pepper. Then add all of the juice from the canned pineapple, and half of the chunks (but if you want this dish really sweet, then by all means put them all in!), the tomato ketchup, balsamic vinegar and honey and squeeze in the lime juice. Stir and then leave to cook for another 8 minutes, giving a quick stir every so often.

>

Sweet & sour pork balls with crunchy peanut rice

(continued)

+ While this cooks, put the peanuts in a pestle and mortar (or use a mug and the end of a rolling pin) and bash them up a bit. Trim and slice the green onions (the green and white bits) and reserve for serving.

+ Check that the rice is ready, add a pat of butter, salt and pepper and the nuts. Stir and cover with the lid to keep warm.

+ Check that the pork balls are piping hot and cooked through by now, and the sauce slightly reduced and thickened, then it's time to serve.

+ Divide the crunchy peanut rice among four plates and top with the pork balls and sauce. Scatter over the green onions and eat!

Tasty tarragon pork steaks with creamy mustard mushroom sauce & green onion champ

Time from start to finish:
25 minutes
Serves: **4**
Equipment: **Kettle, large saucepan and lid, large frying pan, plate, colander**

Champ

2 lbs 3 oz baking potatoes

1 bunch of green onions

4 tbsp butter

Salt and freshly ground black pepper

Pork steaks

Vegetable oil

3 sprigs of fresh tarragon

4–8 pork loin steaks (depending on size)

Salt and freshly ground black pepper

Sauce

3 shallots

11 oz cremini or black poplar mushrooms

2 garlic cloves

2 tbsp butter

½ cup white wine (or Calvados or chicken stock)

1 cup heavy cream

1 tbsp Dijon mustard

Salt and freshly ground black pepper

I don't buy pork steaks that often, but when I need a quick–fix dinner they are always what seem to be left on the meat shelves of my corner store. So to make them into something special, some tarragon and a creamy mushroom sauce are most definitely the order of the day. This champ, for my family, is a winner and makes the usual mashed potatoes into something really special.

+ Put the kettle on. While you wait, peel the potatoes and cut them into about ¾-inch-thick slices. Put them into a large saucepan set on a high heat. Pour the boiled water over, pop the lid on and when the water comes back to the boil, remove the lid and leave to bubble away for 10–12 minutes or until tender.

+ Meanwhile, cook the pork. Put a good drizzle of oil into a large frying pan over a medium to high heat. Pick the leaves from the tarragon and finely chop them. Season the pork steaks on both sides and then rub the tarragon in with your hands. Add the pork steaks to the pan and leave to fry for about 4 minutes on their first side.

+ While they are cooking away, start preparing the sauce ingredients by peeling and finely chopping the shallots. After the pork steaks have been cooking for 4 minutes, flip them over to cook for another 4 minutes. Then finely slice the mushrooms and peel and finely chop the garlic for the sauce. Trim and finely slice the green onions (the green and white bits) for the champ.

+ The pork steaks should now be cooked. They should have no pinkness remaining in their center and be lovely and golden on the outside. Remove them to a plate and cover with aluminum foil to rest and keep warm.

>

Tasty tarragon pork steaks with creamy mustard mushroom sauce & green onion champ

(continued)

+ Melt the butter for the sauce in the pork pan and add the shallots, mushrooms and garlic. Cook for about 5 minutes, stirring every so often, until softened.

+ Meanwhile, check that the potatoes are tender, then drain them well and return them to the pan. Add the butter, a good amount of salt and pepper and mash really well. Stir in the prepared green onions and put the lid on to keep everything warm.

+ Add the white wine (or Calvados or chicken stock) to the now-cooked mushroom mixture, then turn up the heat, scrape any bits from the bottom and leave to bubble away for 2 minutes. Next stir in the cream, Dijon mustard and juices from the resting pork and season with salt and pepper to taste. Bubble away for a final minute or two.

+ Meanwhile, start to plate up. Spoon the champ into the center of each serving plate. Sit two pork steaks on top of each and then spoon the warm mushroom sauce over.

Time from start to finish:
15 minutes
Serves: 4
Equipment: Large frying pan,
large plate, grater, mug or bowl

Pork

Vegetable oil

3 tbsp fennel seeds

Salt and freshly ground black pepper

Four 8-oz boneless pork chops

Salad

1 bag of watercress leaves

4 perfectly ripe, fresh peaches or
14-oz can of peach halves in syrup
or juice

1 bunch of green onions

Small handful of fresh mint

7 oz Stilton or other blue cheese

Dressing

¾-inch piece of fresh ginger

1 big lemon

3 tbsp extra virgin olive oil

Pinch of English mustard powder
(optional)

Squeeze or dab of honey

Salt and freshly ground black pepper

Pan-fried pork chops with a watercress, peach & Stilton salad & a lemon ginger dressing

I am a last-minute food shopper. Round about dinnertime, I am often found wandering around the aisles of my local supermarket, wondering what on earth to make for the family. Again. Last time, the usual suspects were left on the shelves: the ubiquitous ground beef, a package of chicken breasts that looked like it may have encountered a bit of a skirmish during transit to the store and pork chops. I admit, I almost turned my back on the lot of them, clearly rejected by the earlier rush of hungry commuters on their way home, but a flash of tangy, fruity and peppery inspiration hit me. In less than 20 minutes, I was back home, munching on some wonderfully caramelized pork chops with a sumptuously satiating salad.

+ Put a large frying pan on a medium heat with a good drizzle of oil. Scatter the fennel seeds all over a large plate and sprinkle over a little salt and pepper also. Press the pork chops into the mix, turning them over to coat the other side. Make sure they are evenly coated all over as this will give a lovely crust when cooked. Cook them in the pan for about 6 minutes on the first side or until golden brown.

+ As the chops are frying away, scatter the watercress onto one end of a large serving platter. Then halve and pit the fresh peaches or drain the peach halves and halve them again, trim and finely chop the green onions (the green and white bits), rip the leaves from the mint stalks and add them also. Crumble the Stilton or other blue cheese over and then set the salad aside.

>

Pan-fried pork chops with a watercress, peach & Stilton salad & a lemon ginger dressing

(continued)

+ Once the pork chops have cooked for 6 minutes, turn them over and give them another 6 minutes on the other side.

+ Meanwhile, prepare the dressing. Grate the ginger (skin and all) into a mug or small bowl. Squeeze in the juice of the lemon, add the oil, mustard powder (if using), a squeeze or dab of honey and some salt and pepper. Whisk well with a fork and put to the side.

+ When the pork has finished cooking, check to see that the chops are piping hot in the center with no pinkness. Then just turn off the heat and let them sit for a couple of minutes in the pan.

+ Finally, pour the dressing over the salad. Then, arrange the pork chops on the other end of the platter and serve at the table for sharing.

Time from start to finish:
25 minutes
Serves: **4**
Equipment: **Medium sauté pan, kettle, large saucepan with lid, colander, grater**

Olive oil

2 garlic cloves

5 oz cubed pancetta (the one with herbs added already is nice if you can find it)

1 red chilli

Two 14-oz cans of cherry tomatoes (canned chopped tomatoes will work well also)

1 small glass of red wine

3 dabs of tomato purée

2 tsp paprika

2 tsp dried oregano

2 sprigs of fresh thyme

Salt and freshly ground black pepper

12 oz penne pasta

Extra virgin olive oil

1–2 tsp sugar (optional)

To serve

1 bunch of fresh basil

2 oz Parmesan cheese

Dad's penne all'arrabbiata with crispy pancetta & basil

On one of my weekend trips to my dad's house, way back in my youth, he served up a steaming hot bowl of pasta. When I asked him what it was, he said it was "pasta with a hot, angry sauce"—the very tasty penne all'arrabbiata. I love eating at my dad's. His cooking is Italian, warm and welcoming, so it is a pleasure to be able to share this recipe with you.

+ Put a small drizzle of olive oil into a medium sauté pan on a medium heat. Peel and finely chop the garlic while you wait. Once the oil is hot, add the pancetta and let it cook for a few minutes, stirring it from time to time, until it is crisp and golden brown all over. Then add the garlic and cook for 1 minute more, being careful that it doesn't burn.

+ Chop up the chilli, leaving the seeds in if you like it very hot. Throw it into the pan along with the tomatoes, red wine, tomato purée, paprika and oregano. Pick the leaves from the thyme and add them with some salt and pepper, then leave everything to bubble away for about 15 minutes. Stir the sauce now and again so that it does not stick on the bottom.

+ While this cooks, put the kettle on to boil for the pasta. Put a large saucepan on the stove, pour in the boiling water, add the pasta and cook according to the package instructions.

+ Once the pasta is cooked, drain it well and then return it to the pan it was cooked in. Drizzle with some extra virgin olive oil, season with salt and pepper and put the lid on to keep it warm while you finish the sauce.

+ The sauce should now be lovely and rich and thick. Remove it from the heat and give it a taste. If the tomatoes are still a bit acidic, add a teaspoon or two of sugar and return it to the heat for a moment or so. Then taste again, adding a little salt and pepper if you feel it needs it.

+ Add the pasta to the sauce, mix well and then divide among four bowls. I am told that parsley is the traditional herb to top this dish, but I love some ripped-up basil and a little freshly grated Parmesan to finish.

Fish + shellfish mains

Smooth seas do not make a skillful mariner.
African proverb

I have always been a fish lover. Since that first bite of a fish stick covered in bright orange breadcrumbs I knew that fish and I were going to have a long and happy relationship. It is a shame that so many of our waters are being overfished, and not to harp on about the issue, but I always try to buy wild-caught fish wherever possible to ensure that it is sustainably caught and not depleting our stocks. Salmon makes several appearances in this chapter. Its oily flesh goes well with so many things and it is also big enough to stand on its own two feet, with little needed for added flavor. White fish fillets, which often need a bit of a guiding hand to add tang, bite and piquancy to boost their delicate taste, are also out in force, along with their other fish partners in crime, such as tuna and trout.

Time from start to finish:
25 minutes
Serves: 2
Equipment: Blender or food processor, 2 baking trays, large bowl, mug

2 chunky sustainably caught skinless cod fillets

Tapenade

2 oz (¼ cup) pitted black olives

2 tbsp extra virgin olive oil

1 tbsp capers

1 small sprig of fresh rosemary

1 small garlic clove

Salt and freshly ground black pepper

Salad

½ ciabatta loaf

A drizzle of extra virgin olive oil

4 oz cherry tomatoes

½ cucumber

1 red onion

1-oz bunch of fresh basil

Dressing

4 tbsp extra virgin olive oil

2 tbsp sherry vinegar

Pinch of sugar (optional)

Salt and freshly ground black pepper

Tapenade-crusted cod on a bed of crunchy ciabatta, tomato & basil

The Italian side of my family may not look at me with delight as I change the traditional panzanella, which is usually soaked until soggy, to crispy, crunchy croutons that require a noisy eat. Sounds obvious, but I always buy the best extra virgin olive oil I can afford and hide it far away from the family, to be brought out only for dressings and drizzling over sublime dishes such as this.

+ Preheat the oven to 400°F.

+ To make the tapenade, place the olives, oil and capers in a blender or food processor. Run your fingers along the rosemary stalk to remove the leaves, peel the garlic and pop both in. Season with a little salt (remembering the olives are salty) and pepper and blitz until fairly smooth.

+ Place the fish fillets on a baking tray and smear the tapenade over the top. Put in the oven for 10–12 minutes.

+ Then start the salad. Tear the bread into bite-size chunks and toss on a baking tray with a drizzle of oil. Bake in the oven for 6–8 minutes.

+ Meanwhile, cut the cherry tomatoes in half, slice up the cucumber and throw both into a large bowl. Peel and finely slice the onion, pull the basil leaves from their stalks and add both ingredients.

+ Next, make the dressing in a mug. Pour the oil in along with the sherry vinegar and sugar, if using. Season with salt and pepper to taste and whisk the mixture up a little with a fork.

+ Remove the bread from the oven once crisp and golden. Throw it in with the salad, drizzle with the dressing and toss everything together.

+ Check that the fish is cooked; it should be opaque and piping hot all the way through to the center. Once ready, remove it from the oven.

+ Divide the salad between two serving plates. Top with the cod and serve. This ciabatta salad for me is so addictive!

Blackened Cajun cod burgers with aïoli & paprika baked potato wedges

Time from start to finish:
35 minutes
Serves: 4
Equipment: Large baking tray, food processor, large bowl, grater, large frying pan, plate, baking tray

Baked potato wedges

4 large baking potatoes

2 tsp paprika

Good drizzle of vegetable oil

Salt and freshly ground black pepper

1 oz Parmesan cheese

Aïoli

3 garlic cloves

2 medium egg yolks

Big pinch of English mustard powder

1 cup sunflower oil

¼ lemon (optional)

Salad

2 tbsp extra virgin olive oil

1 tbsp white wine or balsamic vinegar

Squeeze or dab of honey

½ tsp English mustard powder

Salt and freshly ground black pepper

4 oz baby spinach leaves

Cod burger

Drizzle of sunflower oil

1 tbsp all-purpose flour

1 tbsp paprika

2 tsp ground cumin

1 tsp chilli powder

Salt and freshly ground black pepper

Few sprigs of fresh thyme (or you can use 2 tsp dried thyme or oregano here instead)

Four 4-oz skinless, sustainably caught cod or pollack fillets

To serve

4 burger buns

Salt and freshly ground black pepper

I am quite partial to home-baked potato wedges, but if you are in a massive hurry, just use frozen French fries sprinkled with a bit of paprika. I won't tell, if you don't!

+ Preheat the oven to 425°F with the top rack at the ready.

+ Cut each potato in half lengthwise and then cut each piece into four or five long wedges. Toss them on a large baking tray with the paprika, oil and some salt and pepper. Arrange them in a single layer and roast in the oven for 30 minutes.

+ Meanwhile, make the aïoli. Peel the garlic cloves and blitz them in a food processor with the egg yolks and mustard powder. With the motor running, slowly add half the oil, drip by drip. Then gradually add the other half in a steady drizzle to make a thick, creamy mayonnaise. Add a squeeze of lemon juice to taste, if using, and set aside.

+ For the salad dressing, mix the olive oil, vinegar, honey and mustard powder together in a large bowl, season with salt and pepper to taste and set aside also.

+ Once the potatoes have been cooking for 15 minutes, pull them out of the oven, finely grate the Parmesan over the top and pop them back in for another 15 minutes.

+ Now, prepare the fish. Put a drizzle of oil in a large frying pan on a medium heat. Put the flour, paprika, ground cumin and chilli powder on a plate with some salt and pepper and toss together. Pick the leaves from the thyme and toss them in (or the dried thyme or oregano).

+ Coat the cod fillets well in the spiced flour, shaking off the excess. Add the fish to the pan and leave to cook for 4 minutes on the first side.

>

Blackened Cajun cod burgers with aïoli & paprika baked potato wedges

(continued)

+ After 4 minutes, flip the fish over to cook on the other side.

+ In the meantime, split the burger buns in half, place them cut side up on a baking tray and put them in the oven for a few minutes to crisp up a little.

+ Put the spinach leaves into the bowl with the dressing and toss.

+ Check that the fish is cooked. The center should be piping hot with shiny, opaque flesh through to the middle. Remove from the heat.

+ Remove the buns and potato wedges from the oven. The wedges should be tender on the inside and crisp and golden on the outside.

+ Sandwich the cod and aïoli between the buns. Serve with the potato wedges and a handful of the dressed leaves. Any spare aïoli will keep for 2 days in the fridge.

Time from start to finish:
30 minutes
Serves: 4
Equipment: Roasting pan, grater,
roasting tray, medium saucepan

Ginger butternut squash
Two 11½-oz bags of prepared
butternut squash
¾-inch piece of fresh ginger
8 garlic cloves
A few fresh sage leaves
Couple of sprigs of fresh rosemary
Extra virgin olive oil
Salt and freshly ground black pepper

Fish
4 chunky, sustainably caught white fish
fillets (such as cod or pollack), skinless
if you don't fancy it
4 tbsp butter
Salt and freshly ground black pepper

Pancetta petits pois
Extra virgin olive oil
4 oz cubed pancetta
11 oz frozen petits pois or peas
Salt and freshly ground black pepper
Small handful of fresh mint leaves
(optional)

Buttered fish with roasted ginger butternut squash & pancetta petits pois

The supermarkets have started stocking prepared butternut squash, which really gets my vote. Although there is something quite satisfying to me about seeing those little amber cubes of yumminess form from that big peanut-shaped veg, when time is of the essence, a little bit of help in a bag goes a long way.

+ Preheat the oven to 400°F.

+ Put the squash into a roasting pan, peel the ginger and finely grate it over, scatter the unpeeled garlic cloves in, rip the sage leaves over and slide your fingers down the length of the rosemary to release the leaves and add them also.

+ Drizzle the whole thing with oil, then season well with salt and pepper and roast in the oven for 25 minutes.

+ Meanwhile, get on with the fish. Lay the fillets skin side down on a roasting tray. Cut the butter into small pieces, reserve a pat, then arrange the rest on top of the fish fillets and season really well with salt and pepper.

+ When the squash has been cooking for 15 minutes, give it a little toss and put the fish in the oven so that the fillets will be ready at the same time.

+ As this cooks, prepare the petits pois. Put a little drizzle of oil in a medium saucepan on a medium to high heat. Once hot, add the pancetta and cook for about 3–4 minutes until crisp and golden. Then throw in the petits pois or peas, the reserved pat of butter and some salt and pepper to taste and let the whole thing cook away for about 5 minutes until the petits pois are tender.

>

Buttered fish with roasted ginger butternut squash & pancetta petits pois

(continued)

+ When everything is cooked, remove the squash and fish from the oven. To check that the fish is done, insert a knife into the thickest part and take a look inside. The flesh should be completely opaque through to the center. The squash should be soft and caramelized on the edges.

+ Divide the squash among four serving plates. Put a piece of fish on top of each with the pancetta petits pois at the side. Drizzle over some oil if you fancy it, rip over the mint leaves, if using, and serve.

Moroccan pesto fish with caramelized onions & haricot beans served with minty pine nut couscous

Time from start to finish:
30 minutes
Serves: 4
Equipment: Medium sauté pan, kettle, blender, medium bowl, large frying pan, plate, colander

Bean mix

Drizzle of vegetable oil

1 large red onion

4 tsp balsamic vinegar

2 tsp sugar

Salt and freshly ground black pepper

14-oz can of haricot beans, chickpeas or flageolet beans

1 oz raisins

Pesto

Large handful of fresh cilantro

Large handful of fresh flat leaf parsley

2 garlic cloves

¼ cup olive oil

2 tsp ground cumin

Couscous

1 cup couscous

Small handful of fresh mint

Handful (about 1 oz) of toasted pine nuts (available from many supermarkets ready toasted)

Large dab of honey (optional)

Salt and freshly ground black pepper

Fish

Drizzle of vegetable oil

2 tbsp all-purpose flour

1 tsp ground cumin

1 tsp ground coriander

1 tsp paprika

Salt and freshly ground black pepper

Four 7-oz chunky, sustainably caught fish fillets like cod or halibut, skin on

This Moroccan pesto is my take on charmoula, a classic North African marinade served with things such as chicken or fish. The flavors are really intense and this is a very filling but healthy dish. The pesto can be made using a pestle and mortar if you don't have a blender—it does take some elbow grease, but it will still work. I freeze the leftover cilantro and parsley stems and use them in soups and stocks for extra flavor.

+ Start with the bean mix. Put a medium sauté pan with a good drizzle of oil on a medium heat. Peel and finely slice the onion and then add to the hot oil with the balsamic vinegar, sugar and some salt and pepper and cook for about 10 minutes, stirring from time to time.

+ Put the kettle on for the couscous and start the pesto while waiting.

+ Rip the leaves from the bunches of cilantro and parsley and peel the garlic cloves. Place all in a blender with the oil and cumin, then blitz to a paste and set aside.

+ Put the couscous in a medium bowl and pour the now-boiled water over to just cover. Cover with plastic wrap and leave to sit for 8 minutes while you cook the fish.

+ Drizzle some oil into a large frying pan over a high heat. Put the flour on a plate and toss through the cumin, coriander, paprika and some salt and pepper. Coat the fillets of fish all over with it, shaking off the excess. Place them, skin side up, into the hot oil and leave to cook for 3 minutes.

+ Now the onions should be lovely and soft. Drain and rinse the beans and stir them into the onions with the raisins and a good amount of salt and pepper. Leave to cook for a few minutes more.

>

Moroccan pesto fish with caramelized onions & haricot beans served with minty pine nut couscous

(continued)

+ After the fish fillets have cooked for 3 minutes, carefully flip them over and leave to cook for another 5 minutes.

+ Check the couscous—it should be nice and tender, so fluff it up with a fork. Rip the mint leaves off the stalks and add them to the couscous with the pine nuts and honey, if using. Season with salt and pepper to taste.

+ Check to see if the fish is cooked by cutting a little slit into the middle—it should be opaque right through to the center.

+ Divide the couscous among four serving plates. Place a piece of fish on top of each, followed by a spoonful of the bean mix and finally some Moroccan pesto.

Time from start to finish:
35 minutes
Serves: 4
Equipment: 2 large sauté pans,
large frying pan, colander

Potatoes

Olive oil

2 lbs 3 oz potatoes

4 sprigs of fresh rosemary

3 garlic cloves

Salt and freshly ground black pepper

Sauce

Drizzle of oil

1 eggplant

2 celery sticks

1 bunch of green onions

1 garlic clove

5 oz sundried tomatoes

14-oz can of cherry tomatoes (canned chopped tomatoes will work well also)

1 tbsp sugar

¼ cup balsamic vinegar

Pinch of chilli flakes (optional)

Handful (about 3 oz) of pitted green olives (optional; I know lots of people don't like them)

Handful (about 2 tbsp) of toasted pine nuts (you can buy them ready toasted from the supermarket)

Salt and freshly ground black pepper

Fish

Drizzle of oil

Four to six 4-oz (approximately) sustainably caught sea bass fillets (any other white fish will work too), skin on

Salt and freshly ground black pepper

Small handful of fresh basil

Pan-fried sea bass with basil & pine nut sweet veggie sauce & rosemary sautéed potatoes

This sweet Spanish sauce is called *samfaina* and is similar to the French ratatouille or the Italian caponata. Each is a type of vegetable stew with varying ingredients depending on the region. The beauty of this sauce is that you can make extra and use it on pasta or bruschetta, or serve it with most meats from pork to lamb. Once you have made it a couple of times, it can be fun to have a play with it, adding your own variants as you fancy.

+ Pour a thin film of oil in a large sauté pan set over a medium heat.

+ Meanwhile, peel the potatoes and cut them into about ¾-inch cubes, strip the leaves from the rosemary stalks and bash the three garlic cloves with the side of a knife to squash them (but leave the peel on).

+ Once the oil is hot, carefully add the potatoes, half of the rosemary and the garlic cloves. Lower the heat and leave to cook gently for about 25 minutes, stirring them from time to time so they cook evenly and don't burn.

+ Pour a drizzle of oil into a large sauté pan and place it on a low to medium heat. Trim and cut the eggplant into bite-size pieces and add to the pan. Adding them to the pan as you go along, trim and finely chop the celery sticks, green onions (both the green and the white bits) and peel and finely chop the clove of garlic. Give everything a good stir and sauté for 1–2 minutes.

+ Roughly chop the sundried tomatoes and add to the pan with the cherry tomatoes, sugar, balsamic vinegar, chilli flakes and green olives, if using, pine nuts and the reserved rosemary.

>

Pan-fried sea bass with basil & pine nut sweet veggie sauce & rosemary sautéed potatoes

(continued)

+ Stir everything together and bring to a simmer, then leave to cook for about 10 minutes, stirring from time to time so that it doesn't stick on the bottom.

+ Drizzle a little oil into a large frying pan on a medium heat. Slash the sea bass skin a few times with a sharp knife and season both sides with salt and pepper. Put the fish skin side down in the pan and leave to cook for 3 minutes.

+ The sauce should now be reduced and the vegetables softened. Taste the sauce, adjust the seasoning if necessary and turn the heat off.

+ Line a colander with paper towels and drain the cooked potatoes. Season them with salt and pepper and leave them to finish draining for a moment.

+ Turn the fish over (the skin should be lovely and crispy) and leave to fry for a further 2 minutes until cooked through.

+ Divide the potatoes among four serving plates, top each with a fillet of sea bass and then spoon the sauce over. Rip the basil leaves over to serve.

Time from start to finish:
25 minutes
Serves: 4
Equipment: Large sauté pan,
pestle and mortar (or a mug
and rolling pin), kettle, large
saucepan with lid, colander

2 tsp fennel seeds

5 oz spicy chorizo

2 sprigs of fresh rosemary

2 garlic cloves

1 red chilli

Olive oil

Two 14-oz cans of chopped tomatoes

1 glass of Cabernet Sauvignon (or
other red wine or a good fish or
chicken stock)

1 tbsp harissa paste (or tomato purée
if you don't like it too hot)

2 tsp dried oregano

11 oz linguine pasta

8 oz sustainably caught peeled shrimp
(preferably raw but cooked will work
too)

Salt and freshly ground black pepper

2 tsp sugar (optional)

Small handful of fresh flat leaf parsley

Shrimp linguine with chorizo & Cabernet tomato sauce

I am a chorizo lover. I cannot get enough of it. I think not a day goes by without me eating some of it. Really! If you can't get your hands on a chorizo "ring," then any flavorful sausage will do. Try some venison sausage or those made with pork and caramelized red onion, which are a great substitute.

+ Put a large sauté pan on a medium heat (with no oil in for the moment). Bash up the fennel seeds using a pestle and mortar (or in a mug with the end of a rolling pin) until lightly crushed and put them in the pan. Cook for 3–4 minutes, tossing them from time to time until they start to release their lovely smell.

+ Meanwhile, slit the chorizo down the side, peel and discard the casing and cut the sausage into chunks. Pull your fingers down the length of the rosemary to release the leaves and then finely chop them. Peel and finely chop the garlic and seed and finely chop the chilli. Add everything to the now sweet-smelling fennel with a little drizzle of oil and cook for 1–2 minutes, stirring.

+ Next add the tomatoes, wine (or stock), harissa paste (or tomato purée) and oregano. Then turn up the heat and leave it to bubble away for about 15 minutes so the sauce can become nice and thick and full of flavor. Give it a stir every so often to prevent it sticking.

+ As this cooks, put the kettle on to boil and then cook the linguine in a large saucepan according to the package instructions.

+ Add the shrimp to the sauce for the last 4–5 minutes of cooking time. If you are using already cooked shrimp, they will take a little less time as you are simply warming them through.

+ Meanwhile, drain the cooked pasta well and return it to the pan, adding a good drizzle of oil and some salt and pepper, then pop the lid on to keep it warm.

>

Shrimp linguine with chorizo & Cabernet tomato sauce

(continued)

+ The shrimp should now be cooked in the sauce. They should be pink and white on the outside and white inside. Taste the sauce, adding some salt and pepper if you think it needs it and a little sugar if it tastes too sharp. If you add sugar, stir it in well and then leave to cook for another minute.

+ Finally, pour the sauce over the pasta, stir well, then divide among four plates, scatter with ripped-up parsley leaves and serve.

Aluminum foil Thai trout with red pepper noodles

Time from start to finish:
30 minutes
Serves: 4
Equipment: Peeler, baking tray, medium wok or sauté pan

Fish

1 bunch of green onions

¾-inch piece of fresh ginger

1 red chilli

1 celery stick

1 carrot

1 garlic clove

½ bunch of fresh cilantro

4 sustainably caught trout fillets (about 4 oz each)

4 tsp soy sauce

4 tsp sesame oil

2 limes

Salt and freshly ground black pepper

Noodles

Sesame oil

1 red pepper

Two 5-oz packages of straight-to-wok medium noodles

2 tbsp soy sauce (optional)

Salt and freshly ground black pepper

Not strictly Thai, but with a nod to its flavors nonetheless. A fun and healthy way to cook a delicious piece of trout, but it can also be replaced with salmon. I've used aluminum foil here, but baking parchment makes a good alternative.

+ Preheat the oven to 400°F.

+ Trim the green onions and then cut them in half, dividing the green and the white bits. Cut each onion in half lengthwise, and set aside. Peel and finely slice the ginger and cut into thin strips. Seed the chilli and cut into long, thin strips also. Halve the celery stick and peel the carrot and cut both into thin, finger-length sticks. Peel and finely slice the garlic and cut the leaves off the cilantro (keeping the leaves and stalks separate).

+ Tear off four 13-inch squares (approximately) of aluminum foil and lay them out individually. Put a piece of trout in the center of each one. Divide all the prepared vegetables among them, scattering them over. Only use the cilantro stalks for now, reserving the leaves for serving. Drizzle the soy sauce and sesame oil over, squeeze in the juice of one of the limes and season with a little salt and pepper.

+ Now wrap the trout up in the foil. Any way will do just as long as the foil is well sealed, but not too taut, so air can circulate and steam the fish. Place the parcels on a baking tray and put in the oven for 12 minutes.

+ A few minutes before the fish is ready, cook the noodles. Put some sesame oil in a medium wok or sauté pan and get it nice and hot. Halve, seed and finely slice the red pepper and then stir-fry for 1 minute. Add the noodles and continue to stir-fry for 2 minutes until they are piping hot. Add some soy sauce to taste if you fancy it and then season well with salt, pepper and a drizzle of sesame oil.

+ Divide the noodles among four serving plates. Remove the trout from the oven and serve in the foil parcels next to the noodles. Quarter the remaining lime and nestle a piece into each one. Serve scattered with the reserved cilantro leaves.

Time from start to finish:
20 minutes
Serves: 2
Equipment: Kettle, small
saucepan, medium saucepan
with tight-fitting lid, small bowl

2 medium eggs

2 cups basmati or long-grain rice

2 tsp curry powder

½ tsp ground turmeric

1 bunch of green onions

Small handful of fresh chives

4-oz package of hot-smoked trout
(it is ready to eat)

4 tbsp butter

Salt and freshly ground black pepper

A few fresh basil leaves

Dressing

2 tbsp low- or full-fat crème fraîche

½ lemon

Salt and freshly ground black pepper

Hot-smoked trout kedgeree with green onions & basil

I am not ashamed to admit that I only discovered hot-smoked trout a few months ago at the supermarket. A great find for a quick and tasty meal. Rub the fish up and down with your fingers before you use it to check for the odd bone that may be there. A truly sumptuous supper dish or one for a decadent breakfast.

+ Put the kettle on to boil for the rice.

+ Place the eggs in a small saucepan and cover with water. Put on a high heat and as soon as the water comes to the boil, let it bubble away for 4 minutes for almost-hard-boiled eggs.

+ Put the rice, curry powder and turmeric in a medium saucepan. Pour over enough boiled water to come about ¾ inch above the rice (roughly 2 cups of water, to be pedantic). Cover with the lid and return to the boil. Then reduce the heat to low and leave to cook for as long as it says to on the package.

+ Meanwhile, slice up the green onions (both the green and the white bits), finely chop the chives and break the fish into bite-size flakes (removing any fine bones that you find) and set aside.

+ Once the eggs are ready, drain them and run them under a cold tap for a moment to stop them from cooking. Peel, cut them into quarters and set them aside.

+ Next, prepare the dressing. Simply spoon the crème fraîche into a small bowl and squeeze the lemon juice in. Season with salt and pepper to taste and stir everything together (it should be quite thin, for drizzling).

+ Check that the rice is tender and fluff it up with a fork. Add the butter and let it melt for a moment before stirring it through. Add the green onions, chives and smoked trout. Season to taste with salt and pepper and gently stir everything together.

+ Divide the rice between two serving bowls, arrange the egg quarters on top and drizzle the dressing over. Scatter the basil over and serve.

Time from start to finish:
10–15 minutes
Serves: 4
Equipment: Large bowl, colander, large frying pan, mug or small bowl

11 oz cherry tomatoes

1 small red onion

Two 14-oz cans of cannellini beans

Large handful of capers

7 oz feta cheese

Sunflower oil

4 large sustainably caught tuna steaks (about ¾ inch thick)

Salt and freshly ground black pepper

Dressing

4 tbsp extra virgin olive oil

2 tbsp balsamic vinegar

Drizzle of maple syrup or honey

Salt and freshly ground black pepper

1 lime

Small handful of fresh mint

Seared tuna steaks with cannellini beans, feta & mint

This is quite a summery dish, but also perfect for those days when perhaps you fancy something a little lighter. You could also try it with rice instead of cannellini beans if you feel like a change.

+ Cut the tomatoes in half and put them into a large bowl. Peel and finely slice up the red onion, drain and rinse the beans, rinse the capers and add these too. Finally, crumble the feta in.

+ Drizzle some oil into a large frying pan and get it nice and hot over a high heat.

+ While this heats up, season the tuna steaks well with salt and pepper, really getting a good amount on. Then lower them into the hot oil. Cook for 1 minute per side for rare, 2 minutes for medium and 3 minutes for well done.

+ Meanwhile, make the salad dressing. Put the oil, balsamic vinegar, maple syrup or honey and salt and pepper into a mug or small bowl and whisk with a fork. Pour over the salad, toss well and divide among four plates.

+ Check that the tuna is cooked to your liking and remove from the heat. Lay a tuna steak on top of each salad portion, quarter the lime and place a piece to the side of each. Then rip over the mint leaves and serve.

Time from start to finish:
15 minutes
Serves: 2
Equipment: Medium frying pan,
large frying pan, sieve, mug

Vegetable oil

Two 4-oz (approximately) sustainably
caught salmon fillets, skin on

Salt and freshly ground black pepper

3 oz spicy chorizo

4 oz asparagus tips (or green beans)

14-oz can of puy or green lentils

2 sprigs of fresh rosemary

Dressing

5 tbsp extra virgin olive oil

3 tbsp balsamic vinegar

1 tbsp maple syrup

Pinch of English mustard powder
or small dollop of Dijon mustard
(optional)

Salt and freshly ground black pepper

Warm salmon & lentils with chorizo, asparagus & a balsamic dressing

I did a big Twitter survey earlier in the year to ask my followers how many frying pans they had. Surprisingly, the answer came back as three on average, which is more than the two I have at home! If you don't have two frying pans, then cook the lentil salad in a medium-sized saucepan. It will just mean a bit more stirring to make sure that everything is cooked, but it will still taste the same. Cook the fish in another pan, skin side down, so the skin crisps up and protects the fish from drying out. I love this at any time of year, when a warm, salady dish is just the thing for my mood.

+ Put a medium frying pan, with a good drizzle of oil in, plus a large frying pan, without oil in, on a medium heat.

+ As the pans heat up, dab the salmon fillets dry with paper towels (this helps the fish skin crisp up nicely) and then season with salt and pepper. Then lower the fish, skin side down, into the pan with hot oil and leave to cook, untouched, for 5 minutes.

+ Meanwhile, make a slit down the side of the chorizo and use your hands to peel the skin off. Then cut the sausage into bite-size chunks and set aside.

+ Lay the asparagus in one bunch on the chopping board and cut off the hard woody ends all in one go. If using green beans, trim the stalk end of each. Toss the asparagus (or green beans) into the hot dry frying pan and leave them to cook for about 2 minutes, tossing all the time so they cook evenly. Then add the chorizo, reduce the heat to low and cook for about 3 minutes, tossing every so often.

+ By now, the fish has probably been frying for about 5 minutes (and the skin is hopefully nice and crispy), so flip it over and leave to cook for another 5 minutes on the other side.

>

Warm salmon & lentils with chorizo, asparagus & a balsamic dressing

(continued)

+ Drain the lentils in a sieve and give them a good rinse. Run your fingers down the length of the rosemary stalks to release the leaves and then finely chop them. Add both ingredients to the chorizo pan and leave to cook for about 5 minutes, stirring every now and again.

+ To make the dressing, place the oil, vinegar, maple syrup and mustard, if using, in a mug, add salt and pepper, then whisk together with a fork and set aside.

+ Now check that the fish is cooked. It should be just opaque and nice and hot in the center. Remove from the heat.

+ Check that the lentils and chorizo are piping hot, season them to taste and then divide them between two plates. Sit a piece of salmon, skin side up, on top of each. Drizzle the dressing over and serve.

Time from start to finish:
30 minutes
Serves: 4
Equipment: Kettle, standard or immersion blender, zester, large saucepan with lid, large frying pan, colander, potato masher or rolling pin

Gremolata potatoes

Large handful of fresh flat leaf parsley
2 garlic cloves
1 lemon
1 tbsp olive oil
1½ lbs baby or new potatoes
Salt and freshly ground black pepper
Pat of butter
Handful of toasted pine nuts (they come ready toasted from the supermarket)

Fish

8 slices of prosciutto or pancetta
Four 4-oz (approximately), preferably skinless, sustainably caught salmon fillets
Salt and freshly ground black pepper
16 good-size fresh sage leaves
Vegetable oil

Salad

1 bag of baby spinach leaves
A drizzle of extra virgin olive oil
A drizzle of balsamic vinegar
1 large handful of sundried tomatoes

Salmon saltimbocca with gremolata potatoes & crispy sage leaves

My dad, who speaks many, many languages, tells me that in Italian *saltimbocca* literally means "to jump in the mouth." So this is "jump in your mouth salmon." It is a traditional European dish usually made with meat wrapped up in sage and prosciutto. Lots of people say that they are not really good at cooking fish. For me, fish cooking is all about practice and experimenting. After a few goes at it, the fish will be just right and then cooking it will begin to come naturally.

+ Put the kettle on to boil for the potatoes. While you are waiting, get started on preparing the gremolata. Rip the parsley leaves off the stalks and place in a blender (an immersion blender works well and is less hassle to wash up!). Peel and add the garlic, grate the lemon zest in and add the oil.

+ Put the potatoes in a large saucepan and pour the boiling water over to cover. Put the lid on, bring back to the boil and then when the pan lid starts to rattle, turn the heat down and leave them to simmer for 15–20 minutes until tender.

+ Now back to the gremolata. Briefly whiz the ingredients in the blender until combined. Season to taste with salt and pepper and set aside.

+ Next, prepare the salmon. Lay two slices of prosciutto or pancetta overlapping lengthwise. Sit a piece of salmon, round side up, near one short edge. Season with salt and pepper and arrange three sage leaves along the length of the fish. Roll the prosciutto or pancetta around the salmon until completely wrapped. Repeat until all four fillets are wrapped (you should have four sage leaves left over, which will get used shortly).

+ Put a large frying pan on a high heat and add a little oil. Once hot, place the fillets in, sage leaf side down, turn the heat to medium and leave them to cook for about 3 minutes.

>

Salmon saltimbocca with gremolata potatoes & crispy sage leaves

(continued)

+ While the fish cooks, throw in the remaining sage leaves. They crisp up in seconds. Then, remove them with tongs or a slotted spoon onto paper towels to drain the excess oil off.

+ Now flip the salmon over and leave to cook for another 6 minutes on the other side.

+ Check on the potatoes—a knife should glide through to the center. Once they are cooked, drain them well and return to the pan. Add some salt and pepper, a big pat of butter, the gremolata, crisp fried sage leaves and the pine nuts. Now I like to use a potato masher or the end of a rolling pin to very gently crush (rather than mash) the potatoes so they are still fairly whole. Put the lid on to keep them warm.

+ To check that the salmon is cooked, cut a little slit underneath through to the center. The flesh should be just turning opaque and pale pink all the way through. If so, remove the pan from the heat.

+ Divide the potatoes among four plates and top with a piece of salmon. For the salad, place a handful of spinach leaves to the side, drizzle with oil and balsamic vinegar, scatter the sundried tomatoes over and serve.

Time from start to finish:
35 minutes
Serves: 4
Equipment: Kettle, grater,
immersion or standard blender
or food processor, large
saucepan with lid, small bowl
or mug, pastry brush, 2 baking
trays, colander, potato masher

2 lbs 3 oz baby or new potatoes

Four 4-oz (approximately) skinless,
sustainably caught salmon fillets

Salt and freshly ground black pepper

2 sheets of phyllo pastry

Extra virgin olive oil

4 vines of cherry tomatoes

Pesto

2 oz Parmesan cheese

Large handful of fresh basil

2 garlic cloves

3 oz toasted pine nuts (you can buy
them ready toasted)

Large handful of curly kale (about
2 oz)

½ cup plus 2 tbsp extra virgin olive oil

Salt and freshly ground black pepper

Phyllo salmon en croute with basil & curly kale pesto & pesto potatoes

I have just bought an immersion blender, which has become my favorite new toy. Put ingredients into a tall pitcher or deep bowl, stick the blender in and blitz. A fabulous invention and the perfect piece of kitchen equipment for a very quick, creamy pesto.

+ Preheat the oven to 425°F, and put the kettle on for the potatoes.

+ Start by making the pesto. Finely grate the Parmesan, pick the leaves from the basil stalks, peel and roughly chop the garlic and put it all into a bowl, blender or food processor. Add the toasted pine nuts, kale and finally the oil, then blitz until smooth, season with salt and pepper to taste and set aside.

+ Put the potatoes in a large saucepan, pour the now-boiled water from the kettle over to cover and add a little salt. Put the lid on, bring back to the boil and leave to bubble away for 15–20 minutes.

+ Season each salmon fillet well with salt and pepper and then spread a teaspoon of pesto on top of each one.

+ Cut the phyllo pastry sheets in half across. Place a salmon fillet, pesto side down, in the middle of one of the pieces of pastry. Pour a little oil into a small bowl or mug and brush it all around the edge of the pastry. Wrap the pastry around the salmon to enclose, just as you would wrap a present. Repeat to make three more parcels, arranging them pesto side up on a baking tray as they are finished.

+ Arrange the vines of cherry tomatoes on another baking tray, season them with salt and pepper and drizzle a little oil over. Bake both salmon parcels and tomatoes in the oven for 12–14 minutes.

+ Meanwhile, check on the potatoes. To test that they are cooked, slide a knife into one of the bigger ones. It should glide through without any resistance.

>

Phyllo salmon en croute with basil & curly kale pesto & pesto potatoes

(continued)

+ When cooked, drain the potatoes and return them to the pan. Add the remaining pesto and then crush the potatoes gently with a potato masher. Season with salt and pepper to taste and then divide among four plates.

+ The salmon should now be cooked through with crisp, golden pastry and the tomatoes softened and just beginning to turn color. Remove them from the oven and place a salmon parcel on top of each pile of potatoes with a vine of cooked tomatoes beside and serve.

Time from start to finish:
25 minutes
Serves: 4
Equipment: Peeler, grater, large frying pan, wok or sauté pan, mug or small bowl

7 oz bok choy

1 bunch of green onions

¾-inch piece of fresh ginger

Sesame oil

Four 4-oz sustainably caught salmon fillets, skin on

Salt and freshly ground black pepper

3 squeezes or dabs of honey

½ cup light soy sauce

Pinch of chilli flakes or powder

1 lime

11 oz straight-to-wok noodles

1 tbsp sesame seeds

Small handful of fresh cilantro leaves

Honey soy–glazed salmon with sesame & ginger noodles & stir-fried bok choy

I realize this recipe is not going to reinvent the wheel, but it is a staple in my house, which comes in handy when my daughter comes home from school, nearly always ravenous from a high-octane day and in need of something quick and tasty with plenty of carbs. Trout fillets, which I have just started using a lot of, make a good alternative to salmon.

+ Trim the bok choy to release the leaves, then rinse and pat them dry with paper towels. Trim and roughly chop the green onions (both the green and the white bits) and peel and grate the ginger.

+ Put a large frying pan and a wok or sauté pan on a medium heat with a small glug of sesame oil in each.

+ Season the salmon fillets well with salt and pepper, and fry them skin side up in the frying pan for 5 minutes.

+ Meanwhile, stir-fry the bok choy, green onions and ginger in the wok or sauté pan for about 3 minutes until the leaves are wilted.

+ While these are frying, quickly put the honey, soy sauce and chilli flakes or powder into a mug or small bowl and whisk everything together with a fork. Quarter the lime and set both aside.

+ Next, carefully flip the fish fillets to cook on the other side for about 4 minutes.

+ Add the noodles and sesame seeds to the vegetables and toss together well, then continue to cook for a few more minutes, keeping everything moving around regularly.

>

Honey soy-glazed salmon with sesame & ginger noodles & stir-fried bok choy

(continued)

+ Turn the heat up on the salmon and pour half of the honey sauce over. Allow to simmer for a couple of minutes, spooning the sauce over the salmon as the mixture thickens and becomes syrupy.

+ Pour the remaining sauce over the noodles, tossing them well, and then season with salt and pepper to taste.

+ The salmon is cooked when it is no longer translucent but an even pale pink through to the center.

+ Divide the noodles among four serving plates. Set a salmon fillet on top of each, drizzle some of the syrupy sauce from the pan over and serve with a wedge of lime and a scattering of cilantro leaves.

Vegetarian mains

Be brave. Take risks. Nothing can substitute experience.
Paulo Coelho

In my teens I went veggie. It was a real "right on" thing to do. A gaggle of girlie crusaders on a meat-free mission, we were the talk of the school and the talk of the tiny town in which I grew up. I do so wish, however, without the risk of blowing my own trumpet, that I had had a few simple recipes like these to cook once a week to get away from the omnipresent baked potato with cheese or pasta with tomato sauce that I used to eat day in, day out! These are a few family favorites that have proven very successful both for casual everyday meals and also for those rare occasions when mates come over for a tasty bite.

Goat cheese, toasted hazelnut & honey quesadillas with arugula salad

Time from start to finish:
15 minutes
Serves: 4 as a snack (or makes 16 triangles for canapés)
Equipment: 2 medium frying pans, pestle and mortar (or a mug and rolling pin), baking sheet, medium bowl

Sunflower oil

4 tbsp (2 oz) roasted chopped hazelnuts (these come ready roasted and chopped at most supermarkets)

Small handful of fresh cilantro

4 corn or wheat tortillas

9 oz goat cheese

4 tsp honey

Salt and freshly ground black pepper

1 bag of wild arugula

Extra virgin olive oil

A drizzle of balsamic vinegar

The other day, my dad rang me to tell me that he had never been a fan of goat cheese and always preferred the blue cheese of Stilton and Dolcelatte. But when he was at one of his many evenings of culture, he had been offered some goat cheese drizzled with honey and had instantly fallen deeply in love with the perfect balance of flavors. So, Dad, this one is for you.

+ Preheat the oven to 225°F.

+ Put two medium frying pans (each wide enough to fit one of your tortillas in flat) on a medium heat with a tiny drizzle of sunflower oil in each.

+ While waiting for the pans to heat up, bash up the hazelnuts with a pestle and mortar (or in a mug with the end of a rolling pin). Pick and roughly chop the cilantro leaves.

+ Place a tortilla in each of the pans and leave to toast for 1 minute. Then crumble over a quarter of the goat cheese and scatter a quarter of the hazelnuts and cilantro over one half of each one. Drizzle a little honey over, season with a little salt and pepper and fold the tortilla over to enclose the filling. Squish them down a bit with a spatula or fish slicer, reduce the heat to low and leave to cook for a minute before flipping over and cooking for 5 minutes on the other side.

+ Slide them out of the pans onto a baking sheet and place in the oven to keep warm while you prepare the other two in the same way.

+ While the last two are cooking, put the arugula leaves into a medium bowl. Drizzle over a bit of olive oil and balsamic vinegar. Scatter in some salt and pepper and then toss everything together.

+ Remove the tortillas from the oven. I like to cut each one into four sections and serve with the dressed arugula as a canapé or starter for a Mexican feast.

Prep time: 25 minutes
Time baking in the oven:
15–20 minutes
Serves: 4
Equipment: Kettle, grater, 2 small
bowls, large saucepan with lid,
large saucepan, medium bowl,
potato masher, 10-inch square
baking dish at least 2½ inches
deep (about 2½ quarts), baking
tray

2 oz Parmesan cheese

2 oz dried plain breadcrumbs

1¼ lbs prepared sweet potato and butternut squash chunks

Pinch of salt

4 sprigs of fresh rosemary

12 sage leaves

Olive oil

12 lasagne sheets

Salt and freshly ground black pepper

4 oz toasted pine nuts (the supermarket sells them ready toasted)

3 oz baby spinach leaves

White sauce

4 oz Parmesan cheese

¾-inch piece of fresh ginger

1¼ lbs ricotta cheese

2 medium egg yolks

Pinch of freshly grated nutmeg

Salt and freshly ground black pepper

Salad

3 tbsp extra virgin olive oil

1 tbsp balsamic vinegar

Pinch of English mustard powder (optional)

Salt and freshly ground black pepper

1 bag of wild arugula

Butternut & sweet potato lasagne with sage, toasted pine nuts & nutmeg

This is one of my stalwart recipes that used to only make an appearance when there was a vegetarian at my house. But then the family began to fall in love with the soft wintry flavors and that creamy white sauce. This white sauce is a shortcut white sauce; everything just gets put in a bowl and stirred—very, very simple and just as tasty as the traditional version.

+ Preheat the oven to 425°F. Put the kettle on to boil for the vegetables.

+ While waiting for that, finely grate the Parmesan for the topping, toss in a small bowl along with the breadcrumbs and set aside.

+ When the kettle has boiled, put the prepared sweet potato and butternut squash chunks in a large saucepan, add a little salt and then pour the boiled water over to cover. Put the lid on, bring back to the boil and then leave to bubble away for 15–20 minutes, until tender.

+ Fill the kettle up with water again and pop it back on to boil.

+ While waiting for the kettle, quickly prepare the herbs for later. Run your fingers down the length of the rosemary stalks to release the leaves, roughly chop them with the sage leaves and set aside in a small bowl.

+ Pour the now-boiled water into a large saucepan, add a drizzle of oil, slip in the lasagne sheets and leave to cook for 5 minutes. (As there isn't loads of liquid in this dish, the lasagne sheets do need a bit of precooking even if they are "no precook" lasagne sheets!)

+ In the meantime, prepare the sauce. Finely grate the Parmesan and peel and grate the ginger. Place both in a medium bowl, add the ricotta, egg yolks and nutmeg, season with salt and pepper, then stir to combine and set aside.

>

Butternut & sweet potato lasagne with sage, toasted pine nuts & nutmeg

(continued)

+ Once the lasagne sheets have cooked for 5 minutes, drain them and put them back in the pan. Drizzle in a little more oil and gently toss them to coat so that the sheets don't stick together.

+ Check that the vegetables are now nice and tender. Drain them well and put them back in the pan. Mash them with a potato masher until smooth and add salt and pepper to taste.

+ Now assemble the lasagne in the baking dish, set on a baking tray. Spread a third of the vegetable mash in the base of the dish. Next, scatter a third of the herbs, pine nuts and spinach leaves over. Then arrange four lasagne sheets on top, cutting to fit if necessary. Spread a third of the white sauce over.

+ Repeat this twice more, giving you three layers, and finally sprinkle the Parmesan breadcrumbs on top. Bake for 15–20 minutes.

+ While that is cooking, prepare the salad dressing by simply mixing the olive oil, balsamic vinegar, mustard powder (if using) and seasoning together in a small bowl.

+ When the lasagne is ready, the pasta will feel tender when pierced through with a knife and the top will be crisp and golden.

+ Cut it into portions, carefully lift out and serve with a handful of arugula drizzled with the dressing.

Prep time: 25 minutes
Time baking in the oven:
20–25 minutes
Serves: 4–6
Equipment: Really large
saucepan or pot with lid, small
saucepan (or small bowl and
microwave), 9-inch springform
pan, baking sheet, sieve, pastry
brush, baking tray

Vegetable oil

1 bunch of green onions

1 garlic clove

1¼ lbs baby spinach leaves

Salt and freshly ground black pepper

4 tbsp butter

7 oz feta cheese

Small handful of fresh dill

7 oz cream cheese

2 oz toasted pine nuts (you can
buy them ready toasted from the
supermarket)

2 oz raisins

3 medium eggs

Big pinch of freshly grated nutmeg

6 sheets of phyllo pastry

4–6 small vines of cherry tomatoes

Extra virgin olive oil

Greek spinach, feta & pine nut pie with dill & crunchy phyllo

An impressive-looking pie. Great hot from the oven or for a packed lunch in the office. Mini ones can be fun to make also: just use a cupcake pan and line each cup with phyllo, add the filling and then top with another piece of this superfine pastry.

+ Preheat the oven to 400°F.

+ Place a really large saucepan or pot with a drizzle of vegetable oil on a medium heat. Trim and finely slice the green onions (the green and white bits), peel and finely chop the garlic and add them to the pan along with the spinach and some salt and pepper. Put the lid on and leave to cook for a few minutes until the spinach is completely wilted, tossing from time to time.

+ Meanwhile, melt the butter in a small saucepan or in a small bowl in the microwave. Use some of it to grease the inside of the springform pan and set aside on a baking sheet.

+ Put the wilted spinach into a sieve and leave it for a few minutes until cool enough to handle.

+ While the spinach cools, crumble the feta cheese into bite-size pieces. Trim the dill stalks off and discard and then roughly chop the leaves.

+ Going back to the spinach mixture, get your hands in and squeeze as much liquid as possible out of it.

+ Return the spinach mixture to the pan (turn the heat off), add the feta, dill, cream cheese, pine nuts and raisins. Crack the eggs in and add the nutmeg and some salt and pepper (not too much salt as the feta is pretty salty). Mix everything together gently. At this stage in the proceedings the mixture won't look like the most beautiful thing in the world, but after a little magic in the oven it will come out well.

>

Greek spinach, feta & pine nut pie with dill & crunchy phyllo

(continued)

+ Open out the phyllo pastry sheets and brush the top one with some of the melted butter. Lay it buttered side up in the prepared pan, pressing it in against the bottom and sides and leaving the excess hanging out over the top. Repeat with three more sheets of pastry, brushing each with butter and laying them not directly on top of one another but overlapping so all of the inside of the pan is covered.

+ Put the spinach mixture inside and spread it out evenly. Fold the excess phyllo pastry inward to enclose the filling. Then lightly scrunch up the remaining two sheets of pastry and arrange them on top, pressing them down lightly, to give a ruffled-effect top. Brush the top with the remaining melted butter and then bake in the oven for 20–25 minutes.

+ Arrange the vines of cherry tomatoes on a baking tray, drizzle a little olive oil over and season well. When the pie has been cooking for about 10 minutes, place the tomatoes in to roast for 10–15 minutes.

+ After 10–15 minutes, remove the tomatoes and pie from the oven. The pie should be crisp and golden on the outside and warmed through. Carefully remove the pie from the pan and use a sharp knife to cut it into four or six wedges.

+ Place a wedge of pie on each serving plate with a vine of roasted cherry tomatoes and serve. This dish is also delicious served cold.

Time from start to finish:
30 minutes
Serves: 4
Equipment: Colander, large bowl,
rolling pin or potato masher (or
food processor), kettle, large frying
pan, medium bowl, heatproof
measuring cup, small bowl

14-oz can of kidney beans

14-oz can of lima beans

1 bunch of green onions

1–2 chillies (depending on how hot
you like it)

1 garlic clove

2 oz sundried tomatoes

Large handful of fresh cilantro

2 oz (¼ cup) dried plain breadcrumbs

2 medium eggs

Salt and freshly ground black pepper

4 oz feta cheese

Sunflower oil

Couscous

1¼ cups couscous

2 tbsp extra virgin olive oil

1½ cups boiled water

5 oz cherry tomatoes

7-oz can of sweet corn

Salt and freshly ground black pepper

Sauce

3 oz (⅓ cup) crème fraîche

Salt and freshly ground black pepper

½ lime

To serve

1 small red onion

1 ripe avocado

Spicy bean burgers with corn couscous & cilantro lime crème fraîche

These burgers can also be served in a bun instead of with the couscous. I like to use a small ciabatta or focaccia roll and just give it a light toasting before serving.

+ Drain and rinse the kidney and lima beans and put them in a large bowl. Using the end of a rolling pin or a potato masher, give the beans a rough mash to break them up a little (or you can give them a really quick pulse in a food processor if you wish).

+ Trim and finely slice the green onions (both the green and the white bits), seed and finely slice the chillies and peel and finely chop the garlic. Finely chop the sundried tomatoes. Pick the cilantro leaves and finely chop half of them (reserving the other half for later). Add all of these to the beans, along with the breadcrumbs, and crack the eggs in. Add a generous amount of salt and pepper and give everything a good mix to incorporate the eggs. Then crumble the feta in and gently fold it through.

+ Quickly put the kettle on to boil for the couscous and put a big glug of sunflower oil in a large frying pan over a medium heat. Then, back to the burgers: divide the mix in four and shape each piece into a burger patty. Add the burgers to the hot pan and leave to cook for 5 minutes.

+ Put the couscous into a medium bowl, drizzle over 1 tablespoon of extra virgin olive oil and pour over 1½ cups of the boiled water from the kettle. Cover tightly with plastic wrap and leave to sit for 8 minutes.

+ Next, prepare the sauce. Finely chop the reserved cilantro leaves and put half in a small bowl with the crème fraîche, salt, pepper and a squeeze of lime juice to taste. Set the sauce and remaining cilantro aside for serving later.

>

Spicy bean burgers with corn couscous & cilantro lime crème fraîche

(continued)

+ Once the underside of the burgers are lovely and crisp and golden, flip them over carefully (as they are softer than regular meat burgers). Drizzle some oil into the pan if dry and leave the burgers to cook on the other side for 5 minutes.

+ Meanwhile, cut the cherry tomatoes in half and drain the sweet corn well. Check that the couscous is tender and, if so, fluff up with a fork. Add the tomatoes, sweet corn and drizzle with the rest of the extra virgin olive oil. Season to taste with salt and pepper and cover again to keep warm.

+ Peel and slice the red onion into rings and set aside for a moment. Cut the avocado in half, remove the pit (see page 45), peel off the skin and cut the avocado into slices.

+ Spoon the couscous onto each serving plate. Check that the burgers are crisp and golden on the other side and remove them from the pan onto the couscous. Arrange the avocado slices and onion rings on the tops of the burgers. Dollop the crème fraîche sauce on top, scatter the remaining cilantro leaves over and serve.

Time from start to finish:
30 minutes
Serves: 4–6
Equipment: 9-inch nonstick
frying pan with lid, peeler,
medium bowl, heatproof rubber
spatula

Sunflower oil

1 medium sweet potato

1 zucchini

1 bunch of green onions

4 oz cremini or black poplar mushrooms

1–2 garlic cloves

1 red pepper

3 oz sliced red jalapeños (you can find them sliced in jars from most supermarkets)

12 medium eggs

Salt and freshly ground black pepper

4 oz canned or frozen and defrosted sweet corn

Salad

1 bag of mixed salad leaves

Extra virgin olive oil

Balsamic vinegar

To serve

Small handful of fresh dill

Small handful of fresh basil

Sweet potato tortilla with jalapeños & dill

You will need a lid for your pan for this spicy Spanish-inspired recipe, but if you don't have one, then cover it tightly with aluminum foil or use a heavy baking tray on top instead. Also, ensure that the pan has a heatproof handle, as it will be going under the broiler.

+ Preheat the oven to 350°F. Put some oil in a frying pan on a low to medium heat. Peel the sweet potato and cut into very thin rounds. Toss into the frying pan, put the lid on and cook gently for about 8 minutes, stirring occasionally.

+ While the potato cooks, trim and finely slice the zucchini, green onions (the green and white bits) and mushrooms and peel and finely slice the garlic. Halve and seed the pepper and slice into strips. Drain the jalapeños well on paper towels and set everything aside for a moment.

+ Check the sweet potato and, when just soft, add the prepared vegetables and sauté for 4–5 minutes until beginning to soften.

+ Meanwhile, crack the eggs into a medium bowl, beat together and season with a good amount of salt and pepper (this dish really needs lots of seasoning). Then, once the vegetables are ready, pour the eggs evenly over and scatter the sweet corn (drained if canned) on top. Turn the heat down to really low, pop the lid on (see my note above) and cook for about 8 minutes.

+ When the tortilla is almost cooked, set the broiler to a medium heat. Once the eggs are cooked at the edge but still a little wet in the middle, remove them from the heat and remove the lid. Slide under the broiler to cook the top for 3–4 minutes. Move the pan to a lower shelf if it is cooking too quickly (you want the egg to cook through to the center, not just the top).

+ Meanwhile, put the salad leaves into a large salad bowl. Drizzle a little olive oil and balsamic vinegar over and set aside for a moment.

+ Once the eggs are just set with a slight wobble in the middle, remove the tortilla from the broiler. Using a heatproof rubber spatula, carefully slide it out of the pan and onto a serving board or plate. Tear some dill and basil leaves over and serve straight to the table with the salad.

Pan-fried mascarpone gnocchi with dreamy basil pesto

Time from start to finish:
45 minutes
Serves: 4
Equipment: Grater, blender or food processor, medium bowl, 2 large frying pans, fish slicer

Pesto

1 oz Parmesan cheese

1 garlic clove (preferably roasted)

Two 1-oz packages of fresh basil

¼ cup extra virgin olive oil

2 oz toasted pine nuts (they come ready toasted from the supermarket)

Salt and freshly ground black pepper

Gnocchi

4 oz Parmesan cheese

Small handful of fresh thyme sprigs (or 1 tbsp dried oregano)

12 oz mascarpone

2 cups all-purpose flour, plus extra for dusting

2 medium eggs

Salt and freshly ground black pepper

Olive oil

4 tbsp butter

To serve

1 bag of wild arugula

1 oz toasted pine nuts

1 lemon

Freshly ground black pepper

I first had gnocchi in an Italian restaurant near my house and I had to find out all about it: where it was from, how it was made and its variations. The owners told me they used mashed potatoes and other ingredients to make the teeny pillows of heaven. I really wanted to put them in this book, but I needed a quicker method, so I threw tradition to the wind and made up my own version with flour and mascarpone, drawing on British dumplings for inspiration. These are great to make in bulk and freeze raw. Also try experimenting with other sauces, such as the all'arrabbiata on page 156.

+ First, prepare the pesto. Finely grate the Parmesan and put it in a blender or food processor. Peel the garlic, tear the leaves from the basil and add both with the oil and pine nuts. Blitz to a paste, season and set aside.

+ Now, for the gnocchi. Finely grate the Parmesan and put it in a medium bowl. Pick the thyme leaves and add them (or the oregano) with the mascarpone, flour, eggs and salt and pepper. Mix to make a soft dough. Turn it out onto a lightly floured surface and knead to form a smooth ball.

+ Divide the mixture into three sections and roll each out into a sausage about 2 feet long. Cut each into ¾-inch pieces to give about 30 (90 in total). Halfway through, put two large frying pans on a medium to high heat with a drizzle of oil and pat of the butter in each. Divide the gnocchi between the two pans and turn the heat down low. Leave the gnocchi to cook on one side for a minute, then carefully turn them over with a fish slicer. Cook for 4 minutes more, continuing to turn them every so often until they are crisp and golden all over and warmed through. If all the gnocchi don't fit in your pans, then put the cooked ones in a bowl, cover with aluminum foil to keep warm and cook the remainder, adding more oil and butter as necessary.

+ Once all the gnocchi are cooked, toss them with the pesto and arugula until evenly coated. Then, divide them among four plates. Scatter the pine nuts over. Add a good squeeze of lemon juice, a grind of pepper and serve.

Cakes + desserts

Everything in moderation . . . including moderation.
Julia Child

For me, my life is not complete without the occasional bit of cake or dessert: soft, squidgy chocolate cake, no-bake cheesecake or a citrusy, crunchy lemon and lime drizzle cake. There is nothing quite like that moment when a cake or dessert (made with such care and attention) is brought to the table to awaiting mouths, to be met with oooooohs and ahhhhhs and doesn't-that-look-lovelys. Making cakes for me is cathartic—watching the eggs, sugar, flour and other such basic ingredients combine to create something that usually becomes the sparkling jewel in the entire meal's crown.

Prep time: **15 minutes**
Chilling time: **10 minutes in the freezer (or 20 minutes in the fridge)**
Time baking in the oven:
25 minutes
Makes: **8 pies**
Equipment: **Large baking sheet, medium bowl (if using store-bought applesauce), zester, rolling pin, pastry brush, sieve**

1¾ lbs Bramley applesauce (see page 295 if making yourself, but store-bought is fine too)

If using store-bought applesauce
1 lemon
1 tsp ground cinnamon
1 tsp ground ginger

Pastry
Small handful of all-purpose flour
1 lb puff pastry (store-bought, or to make your own see page 266)
1 medium egg
Confectioners' sugar, for dusting

To serve
Softly whipped cream, ice cream or crème anglaise (see page 292)

Little warm Bramley apple pies or "chaussons aux pommes"

Store-bought applesauce is fine to use. In fact, it is a great time saver when in a hurry; ditto for the pastry. There may be some leftover pastry here, which can be wrapped up and frozen and kept for a month. Or roll it out into a rectangle, spread on either tapenade or chopped sundried tomatoes, roll up like a jelly roll, then slice in ⅜-inch slices and bake. Hey presto—easy little canapés.

+ Line a large baking sheet with baking parchment and set aside.

+ If you are using store-bought applesauce, just empty it into a medium bowl and finely grate the lemon zest over. Add the cinnamon and ginger, stir everything well to combine and set aside. If using your own homemade applesauce, make sure it is completely cool before using (and simply skip to the next step).

+ Put some flour on the work surface and roll the pastry out to a 16-inch square. Keep the pastry moving around as you roll so it does not stick, adding more flour underneath if need be. The pastry will be really nice and thin. Then cut out eight 4 x 8-inch rectangles (cut the pastry in half and then across the opposite way into quarters) and arrange them on the baking sheet.

+ Crack the egg into a mug, whisk it lightly and then, using a pastry brush, brush a ⅜-inch border around the edge of each pastry rectangle (and hang on to the remaining egg for later). Then, using up all of the applesauce, put a few dollops of it on one half of each rectangle (inside the border). Stuff as much of the applesauce as you can inside the pastries—otherwise they won't look nice and plump when they're cooked. Fold the other half of the pastry over the applesauce and use your fingers to press the edges down to seal. Press in good and tight to the applesauce so everything is nice and cozy.

>

Little warm Bramley apple pies or "chaussons aux pommes"

(continued)

+ Put the pies in the freezer for 10 minutes to firm up (or the fridge will do just fine if you have double that time to spare). Preheat the oven to 400°F.

+ Once the pies are firm, remove them from the freezer, brush liberally with the remaining egg and then mark the top of the pastries with a sharp knife in whatever pattern you like. I like to do the outline of an apple. Put them in the oven for about 25 minutes.

+ Once cooked, the pastry should be crisp and golden brown, so remove the pies from the oven. Leave to cool a bit before eating (that applesauce gets superhot!). I really love to eat these while they are nice and warm, but they are very tasty served cool too. Either way, give a sift of confectioners' sugar over them before tucking in with a little softly whipped cream, ice cream or crème anglaise.

Time from start to finish:
40 minutes
Serves: **4**
Equipment: **Large roasting pan, zester, small bowl, grater**

4 ripe peaches or nectarines

4 fresh figs

2 ripe pears

1 cup dark rum (or port or apple juice for something nonalcoholic)

3 tbsp soft light brown sugar

1 vanilla bean (or a couple of drops of vanilla extract)

1 cinnamon stick

2 sprigs of fresh rosemary

1 orange

To serve

9 oz low- or full-fat crème fraîche

¼ cup confectioners' sugar

Handful (about 1 oz) of toasted hazelnuts (they come ready toasted from the supermarket)

Whole nutmeg

Rum punch roast pears, figs & peaches with toasted hazelnuts & vanilla crème fraîche

This recipe has all sorts of parts to it that reflect my heritage and what I am about. The rum punch is a gentle nod to my Caribbean island girl roots and the peaches and pears point to the fact that a huge part of me is quintessentially English.

+ Preheat the oven to 400°F.

+ Halve the peaches or nectarines and discard the pits, halve or quarter the figs, depending on size, and then quarter the pears lengthwise and remove their cores. Arrange all of the fruit pieces, cut side up, in a large roasting pan.

+ Next, drizzle over the rum (or port or apple juice) and scatter the sugar over. Use a sharp knife to split the vanilla bean in half lengthwise and add half of the bean to the fruit, reserving the other half for later (or add a couple of drops of vanilla extract, if preferred).

+ Snap the cinnamon stick in half and throw it in with the leaves from the rosemary sprigs. Finely grate the zest of the orange all over the fruits, then halve it and squeeze the juice over also.

+ Cover the pan tightly with aluminum foil and roast in the oven for 30 minutes, removing the foil after 20 minutes (and giving the fruit a quick baste with the juices before putting it back in).

+ Spoon the crème fraîche into a small bowl and sift the confectioners' sugar over. Scrape the vanilla seeds from the reserved half of the vanilla bean and add them too (or a couple of drops of vanilla extract). Stir everything together to just combine.

>

Rum punch roast pears, figs & peaches with toasted hazelnuts & vanilla crème fraîche

(continued)

+ Remove the fruit from the oven once it's cooked. It should be deliciously soft and sticky and the sauce rich and syrupy.

+ Spoon the fruit onto warmed serving plates. Each person will have two peach halves, two or four fig pieces, depending on how they were cut, and two pieces of pear. Dollop some crème fraîche to the side, add a sprinkling of toasted hazelnuts, finely grate a little nutmeg over the top and serve.

Time from start to finish:
10 minutes (if using store-bought meringues; see page 225 for homemade)
Serves: 6
Equipment: Large bowl and hand whisk or handheld electric mixer or freestanding electric mixer set with the whisk attachment, small bowl and microwave (or small pan) (optional)

1 ginger ball (this comes in syrup and can be found in the baking section of the supermarket) or 1–2 pieces of crystallized ginger

½ vanilla bean (or a couple of drops of vanilla extract)

1 cup plus 2 tbsp whipping or heavy cream (keep it in the fridge until you need it so it whips up more easily)

¼ cup confectioners' sugar

12 meringue nests (store-bought, or for homemade see page 225)

11 oz blackberries

2 oz white or dark chocolate, to drizzle (optional)

A few fresh mint leaves

Neat-and-tidy Eton mess with blackberries & ginger whipped cream

There are times when I feel that the kitchen is my haven and wild horses could not drag me away from it. It is then that I make these white crispy cradles from scratch. At other times (which, if you are like me, seem to occur far too often these days), I am dashing around the kitchen to pull off a dessert in 20 minutes flat. So I have given the choice of both to alternate at your will. And the fruit and cream spiked with peppery ginger is almost good enough to eat on its own!

+ If you are using store-bought meringues, then carry straight on with the recipe. If you are going to make the meringues from scratch, then turn to page 225 for the recipe and while they are cooking turn back to this page to make the filling.

+ Finely chop the stem ginger ball and then split the piece of vanilla bean open and remove the seeds. Set both aside.

+ Pour the cream into a large bowl and sift in the confectioners' sugar. Whip it up until it just begins to thicken. A handheld or freestanding electric mixer or a standing electric mixer makes light work of this, but you can do it with a hand whisk and plenty of elbow grease.

+ Gently stir the ginger and vanilla seeds (or extract) in with as few stirs as possible.

+ Arrange six of the meringues on a large serving platter or cake stand and, using half the cream, put a blob on each one. Arrange the blackberries on the cream, and then use the rest of the cream on top. Set the remaining meringues on top, pretty side up.

+ For something really fancy, melt the white or dark chocolate in a small bowl either in 30-second blasts in a microwave or set over a small pan of simmering water. Use a small spoon or fork to drizzle it back and forth across the meringue stacks. Rip over some mint leaves and serve.

Prep time: **20 minutes**
Time baking in the oven:
30–40 minutes
Cooling time: **20–30 minutes**
Makes: **12 meringues**
Equipment: **3-inch saucer or bowl, 2 large baking sheets, medium bowl and hand whisk or handheld electric mixer or freestanding electric mixer set with the whisk attachment, piping bag fitted with 2D or star nozzle (optional)**

4 medium egg whites (at room temperature) or ½ cup pasteurized egg whites (I found them in the milk section of the supermarket)

Squeeze of lemon juice

¾ cup plus 2 tbsp sugar

1 tsp cornstarch

Homemade meringues

This is my fail-safe meringue recipe, used here for these little nests. This works well for a pavlova too or for the meringue on top of a lemon meringue pie. You could try something different and stir in a couple of handfuls of roasted chopped hazelnuts to add crunch.

+ Preheat the oven to 250°F. Using a 3-inch-diameter template (like a saucer or bowl), mark out 12 circles on two sheets of baking parchment. Turn them facedown onto two large baking sheets and set aside.

+ Now for the meringues. Get a really clean medium bowl. If it is not spotlessly clean, the egg whites may not whip up properly. This goes for all the equipment.

+ Put the egg whites into the bowl, squeeze the lemon juice in and then whisk the whites to a medium peak. A handheld electric mixer or freestanding electric mixer is best for the job, but you can do this with a hand whisk and plenty of elbow grease. To test, lift the whisk out of the meringue with some of the white foam on the end. Then point it upward and the bit of meringue on the end should flop over.

+ Next, add a spoonful of the sugar to the meringue and whisk really hard until all of the sugar has dissolved and the mixture starts to look a bit shiny. Then add the remaining sugar gradually, while whisking all the time, until the mixture becomes really shiny and very stiff.

+ If you perform the whisk trick at this time, the peak would be almost straight up in the air with only a hint of a flop. If you are using egg white from a carton, the peak will still remain quite floppy, but the mixture will be very shiny and stiff.

+ Finally, whisk in the cornstarch for a second or two until smooth. This gives the meringue a bit of an inner chewiness.

>

Homemade meringues

(continued)

+ Put tiny dots of the meringue on the four corners of the baking sheets to secure the paper. You can then dollop blobs of the mixture into each of the 12 circles on the paper and spread each one out to the circle edge with the back of a spoon. I like to put either a number 2D or a star nozzle (available on the Internet and from some cake shops) in a piping bag and fill the bag with the meringue mixture. Then, starting in the center of each circle, holding the piping bag vertically and squeezing it gently, go round and round until the entire circle is filled to give a pretty flat rose shape. When you come to the end of the rose shape, keep the bag moving but stop squeezing it. This will give a neat end to the rose. Repeat with the rest of the mix and then bake in the oven for 30–40 minutes.

+ If the meringues crack or weep, just turn the oven down by 25° or so. Once the meringues are ready, remove them from the oven and allow them to cool.

Prep time: **30 minutes**
Time to set: **30 minutes in the fridge (or 15 minutes in the freezer)**
Makes: **4 very hefty portions**
Equipment: **Small saucepan, mug or small bowl, large bowl and handheld electric mixer or freestanding electric mixer fitted with the whisk attachment (optional), four ⅔-cup glasses or ramekins, fine sieve**

¾ cup heavy cream

5 oz dark chocolate (at least 70% cocoa solids)

2 oz milk chocolate

3 very fresh medium eggs

3 tbsp sugar

2 oz fresh raspberries

2 tsp confectioners' sugar, to decorate

Chocolate mousse with raspberries

I have made this mousse with many different types of chocolate. My favorite combo is the one given here, but 4 oz of each for those with a slightly sweeter tooth is also chocolate perfection. Use the freshest eggs you can find as they will be eaten raw (so best not to serve this dish to the very young, infirm or ladies who are pregnant). When making this, I challenge you not to eat almost a whole portion before it goes into the glasses!

+ Put the cream in a small saucepan on a medium heat and leave to warm up.

+ Meanwhile, snap or chop the chocolate into small pieces. Once the cream is just starting to steam, remove it from the heat and add the chocolate. Don't stir it (tempting though it is!), but just leave it to sit and melt for about 5 minutes or so.

+ In the meantime, separate the eggs, putting the yolks in a mug or small bowl and the whites in a large, spotlessly clean bowl (or the bowl of a freestanding electric mixer, if using).

+ Whisk the whites, preferably using a handheld electric mixer (or the freestanding electric mixer), until they reach a medium peak. To test, stick the whisk or beater into the egg white and then flip it handle side down. The peak should look like a floppy Noddy's hat, not standing up straight at attention. If so, then add 1 tablespoon of the sugar and whisk it up again until the whites begin to become shiny. Then, while continuing to whisk, add another tablespoon of the sugar. Make sure that the whites are whisked up well and all of the sugar is dissolved before whisking in the final tablespoon of sugar.

+ Meanwhile, have a look at the chocolate. It may not appear to, but the chocolate will most likely be melted by now, so stir everything together. Then add the egg yolks and stir to combine.

>

Chocolate mousse
with raspberries

(continued)

+ Once the whites are lovely and thick and glossy, stir in a spoonful of the chocolate mixture. This will loosen the whites up a bit and make it easier to manage the next step. Gradually pour all of the chocolate into the egg whites and then gently fold them together. Try not to be too heavy-handed or overmix this, as it is good to keep as much air as possible in it.

+ Divide among the four ⅔-cup glasses or ramekins and lightly press the raspberries into the tops. Cover each one loosely with plastic wrap and then pop in the fridge for 30 minutes or so to firm up (or if you want to eat them ASAP, put them in the freezer for 15 minutes). These can be made in the morning for a dinner party in the evening. If they are in the fridge for that long, I like to take them out 15 minutes or so before I need them so that they are not too cold for the guests.

+ Just before serving, decorate the top of each mousse with confectioners' sugar. I hold a piece of paper with a straight edge quite closely over the part I don't want the confectioners' sugar to be on and then dust away (through a fine sieve) to give a nice detail over about a third of the top.

Prep time: 15 minutes, plus 5
minutes if using the sugar syrup
Time baking in the oven:
25 minutes
Cooling and assembly time:
25 minutes
Makes: 12 mini cakes
Equipment: 12-cup muffin pan,
12 muffin/cupcake paper liners,
large bowl, mechanical ice
cream scoop (optional), small
saucepan (if making sugar
syrup), large wire rack, pastry
brush (optional), small bowl,
large bowl, fine sieve, hand
whisk, small bowl and microwave
or medium saucepan

Sponge cake

1 cup plus 2 tbsp soft salted butter

¾ cup sugar

5 medium eggs (at room temperature)

1¾ cups self-rising flour

1 tsp baking powder

Pinch of salt

½ vanilla bean (or a couple of drops
of vanilla extract)

Sugar syrup (optional)

⅓ cup sugar

½ cup water

Filling

1 cup plus 2 tbsp whipping or heavy
cream

2 tbsp confectioners' sugar

½ vanilla bean (or a couple of drops
of vanilla extract)

To assemble

6 oz (¾ cup) good strawberry jam

3 oz white chocolate, for drizzling

12 strawberries, preferably with a little
bit of stem attached (but stemless is
fine too)

Strawberry & cream mini cakes with chocolate drizzle strawberries

On the show, I am always making things in my standing electric mixer. Someone pointed out that not everyone has a standing mixer and would I mind writing the recipe for people who make it by hand. So here it is. Among other things, the secret to a good cake is to make sure the ingredients are all at room temperature. If your eggs are fridge cold, put them in a bowl filled with warm water for a few minutes to heat them up a bit. I like my cakes to be really moist, so I've included a recipe for sugar syrup. This is optional, though, and the cakes will taste just fine without it if you choose not to include this step.

+ Preheat the oven to 350°F. Line a 12-cup muffin pan with paper liners and set aside.

+ First, get started on the sponge cake. Put the butter in a large bowl. If it is not soft, then either grate it in or get your hands in and really squash and squeeze it for a moment or two. Messy? Yes. Fun? Absolutely!

+ When the butter is soft, add the sugar. Use a wooden spoon to really beat it all together well. It won't go that fluffy by hand, but it will go a bit lighter and everything should be very soft.

+ Add the eggs (I admit I just chuck them all in at once) and then beat the whole thing like mad for a couple of minutes until it all combines. The strength of your beating will ensure that everything comes together nicely. Now add the flour, baking powder and salt. Split the vanilla bean open with a small knife, scrape the seeds out of one half and add them too (or the vanilla extract). Then mix everything together so it is just combined.

>

Strawberry & cream mini cakes with chocolate drizzle strawberries

(continued)

+ Now, using two spoons (or a mechanical ice cream scoop if you have one), divide the mixture among the 12 paper liners and then put them into the oven to bake for 25 minutes.

+ If you've decided to use the sugar syrup for extra-moist cakes, then make it now. Put the sugar in a small saucepan with ½ cup of cold water and place on a medium heat. Allow the sugar to dissolve, stirring from time to time. Then, once the sugar has dissolved, turn up the heat and boil the syrup for 2 minutes before removing and setting aside.

+ The sponge cakes are cooked if they spring back when touched and should be a rich golden brown. Remove them from the oven and leave to cool in the pan for a few minutes until cool enough to handle.

+ Remove their paper liners and cut the cakes in half across the equator. Arrange the bottoms and tops, cut side up but separate from each other, on a large cooling rack. This will also help them to cool down completely much more quickly. If you are using the (optional) sugar syrup, then brush the cakes liberally with it as soon as they have been cut in half.

+ Once they are almost cool, prepare everything for assembly. Spoon the strawberry jam into a small bowl, give it a good stir to loosen it up and set aside.

+ Next put the cream into a large bowl and sift the confectioners' sugar in. Scrape the seeds out of the other half of the vanilla bean and add them too (or the vanilla extract, if using). Whisk it up until it just begins to thicken and then set it aside.

+ Now, melt the white chocolate for drizzling. Break up the chocolate and put it in a small bowl. Melt it in the microwave in 30-second blasts, stirring after each blast. Otherwise, put the bowl over a pan of simmering water, making sure that the bottom of the bowl does not touch the water as this can make the chocolate go grainy and lumpy.

+ Assemble once the cakes are completely cool. Put a dollop of strawberry jam on each of the cake bottoms, followed by a dollop of the cream. Put the other halves on top and then put another dollop of the cream on top of that. Place an unhulled strawberry on each mini cake. Finally, use a fork to drizzle the melted white chocolate over.

+ Arrange on a large platter or cake stand or lift straight onto small plates and serve.

Prep time: 20 minutes (if using ready-rolled pastry)
Time baking in the oven: 35–45 minutes
Serves: 6
Equipment: 4 x 13-inch rectangular fluted loose-bottomed flan pan (at least 1 inch deep), rolling pin, baking sheet, medium bowl and handheld electric mixer or freestanding electric mixer fitted with the paddle attachment, colander, small bowl, fine sieve

Pastry

13-oz package of pie dough

or

1-lb package of shortcrust pastry

or

1 lb homemade sweet shortcrust pastry (see page 269)

Almond filling

½ cup soft butter

⅓ cup sugar

4 oz ground almonds

3 tbsp all-purpose flour, plus a little extra for dusting

1 medium egg

1 tbsp amaretto liqueur

Topping

14-oz can of pear halves or 4 very ripe soft pears

Cream

9-oz tub of mascarpone

1 ginger ball (the type in syrup) or 1–2 pieces of crystallized ginger

½ vanilla bean (or a couple of drops of vanilla extract)

2 tbsp confectioners' sugar

To decorate

1 tsp confectioners' sugar

Small handful of fresh mint

Pear, almond & amaretto tart with ginger mascarpone cream

I have had my eye on this little tart for some time. I first consumed one like this in all its ambrosial splendor in a supermarket café in France. Determined to create one like it at home, I set about trying to make it from memory. Being challenged many times over to find pears at the peak of their ripeness, I discovered that their canned counterparts came to the rescue with very pleasing results.

+ Preheat the oven to 350°F.

+ Unravel the rolled store-bought pastry (if using) and line a flan pan with it. Roll it out a touch more, if necessary, to fit in perfectly. If using a block of store-bought or ball of homemade pastry, then roll out to just bigger than the pan on a floured surface and use in the same way. Either way, be really careful not to stretch the pastry or pull it, as this will make it shrink in the pan when it cooks.

+ Try and get the pastry right into the fluted edges of the pan. I use a wooden spoon handle dipped in some flour to ease the pastry into the "flutes." Cut off the excess pastry with a sharp knife and then set the pan on a baking sheet and pop in the fridge to harden up a bit while you prepare the filling.

+ Mix the butter and sugar together in a medium bowl either by hand or using a handheld electric mixer (or in a freestanding electric mixer) until it is really soft and well combined. Then beat in the ground almonds and flour. Crack the egg in, add the amaretto liqueur and then beat it hard so everything is combined. Remove the lined pan from the fridge and add the almond filling, spreading it out evenly so it is nice and smooth on top.

>

Pear, almond & amaretto tart with ginger mascarpone cream

(continued)

+ Drain the canned pears well in a colander and then on paper towels. Or peel, halve and core the fresh pears, if using.

+ Arrange the pear halves, cut side down, on the almond filling. If you lay the tart pan running from left to right in front of you, then lay a pear half in it pointing away from you, then the next one pointing toward you and so on, so they are in an alternating pattern and all fit in perfectly.

+ Bake in the oven for 35–45 minutes or until the filling is nicely puffed up and golden.

+ About 5 minutes before the tart is ready, put the mascarpone in a small bowl. Finely chop the ginger, split the vanilla bean open and scrape out the seeds and add them (or the vanilla extract) to the bowl. Sift the confectioners' sugar in and then stir everything together gently. Just give it a few stirs; otherwise the mascarpone may split and go grainy. Set aside for serving.

+ Check that the tart is cooked. The pastry will be crisp and golden and the almond filling should have puffed up a little around the pears and be golden brown and spongy. Stick a skewer or point of a sharp knife into the center of the filling to check that it is done. It will be just a little damp from the moisture of the pears, but shouldn't be really wet like the original raw mixture.

+ Once cooked, remove from the oven and leave to cool in the pan for a few minutes before carefully removing it from the pan. I set the pan on two upturned glasses and drop the side of the pan down to reveal the tart. Then simply slide the tart off the base onto a long serving platter.

+ To decorate, hold the base of the pan quite close to the tart to cover all but about ¾ inch of one of the long edges. Then dust half of the confectioners' sugar over through a fine sieve. Repeat with the other long edge. Sprinkle over some picked mint leaves and serve warm with the ginger mascarpone cream. This is also really good served cold.

Prep time: 20 minutes
Chilling time: 30 minutes in the freezer (or 4 hours in the fridge)
Serves: 12
Equipment: Large saucepan, plastic food bag and rolling pin (or food processor), 9-inch springform pan (at least 3 inches deep), 2 large bowls, zester, fine sieve, handheld electric mixer (optional), offset spatula (optional)

6 tbsp butter

9 oz digestive biscuits or graham crackers

2 tbsp soft light brown sugar

1¾ lbs cream cheese

1 lemon

1 vanilla bean (or a couple of drops of vanilla extract)

3¼ cups chilled heavy cream

⅓ cup confectioners' sugar

Doorstop vanilla cheesecake

This is my ultimate vanilla cheesecake. It's not too sweet, but if you prefer it sweeter, then ¼ cup of extra confectioners' sugar should do the trick, but taste it before it goes into the pan to make sure you're happy. The lemon zest gives it a nice freshness without necessarily tasting lemony. If you want a lemony edge to it, simply add the zest of one or two more lemons, again tasting it before using.

+ Put the butter in a large saucepan over a low heat and leave to melt. Place the digestive biscuits or graham crackers in a plastic food bag, seal it up and bash them with a rolling pin to make fine crumbs. It's also quicker and easier to blitz them in a food processor if you have one.

+ Add the crushed biscuits to the now-melted butter, add the soft light brown sugar and mix together well. Then evenly press the mixture into the bottom of the cake pan, really packing it in tight by pressing it down with your hand or the back of a spoon. Place in the fridge to firm up while you make the topping.

+ Put the cream cheese in a large bowl and finely grate the lemon zest over. Halve the vanilla bean, scrape out the seeds and add them (or the vanilla extract) too. Mix together well to loosen the mixture slightly.

+ Pour the heavy cream into a large bowl and sift in the confectioners' sugar. Whisk it, by hand or with a handheld electric mixer, to almost the same consistency as the cream cheese, just a little looser.

+ Then add the cream to the cream cheese mixture and mix everything gently, with as few stirs as possible. Scrape it onto the biscuit base and smooth the top with the back of a spoon or an offset spatula.

+ Cover with plastic wrap and put it in the freezer for about 30 minutes until just set. You can, of course, set this in the fridge, but it will take

>

Doorstop vanilla cheesecake

(continued)

considerably longer (about 4 hours). Handy to know if making in advance, though obviously you wouldn't want to leave it in the freezer for too long!

+ Remove the cheesecake from the fridge/freezer 10 minutes or so before serving to bring to room temperature a bit (but don't leave it out for too long as it will go too soft).

+ Serve and enjoy, enjoy, enjoy.

Dulce & banana cake

Prep time: **30 minutes**
Time baking in the oven:
35–45 minutes
Makes: **9 big squares or
12 small ones**
Equipment: **8-inch square cake
pan, small saucepan, baking
tray (optional), large bowl and
handheld electric mixer or
freestanding electric mixer fitted
with the whisk attachment, large
flat plate**

Sticky topping

4 tbsp butter, plus extra for greasing
¼ cup soft light brown sugar

Sponge cake

Handful of pecans (about 2 oz)
(optional)
10 tbsp soft butter
¾ cup soft light brown sugar
4 medium eggs (at room temperature)
½ vanilla bean (or a couple of drops
of vanilla extract)
¾ cup self-rising flour
½ cup whole wheat flour
1 tsp baking powder
3 tsp ground ginger
1 tsp ground cinnamon
1 tbsp molasses
Pinch of salt

Bananas

2 small firm bananas
1 tbsp Calvados (optional)

To serve

Crème anglaise (see page 292),
Salted caramel toffee sauce (see page
294), or softly whipped cream or
ice cream

A superquick, supertasty banana sheet cake. I am
sure most of you know that *dulce* is Italian for "sweet."
I came up with this one night sitting in front of the telly
half-watching TV. I thought of my old job in fashion,
I thought of a famous Italian design duo and, well, then
I thought up the name of this cake!

+ Preheat the oven to 350°F, with the middle shelf at the ready. Grease
and line an 8-inch square cake pan with baking parchment and grease
again.

+ First, make the sticky topping. Place the butter and soft light brown sugar
in a small saucepan over a medium heat. Once the butter is melted,
turn up the heat and let the mixture bubble away for a few minutes until
it begins to thicken slightly. Stir it frequently so it does not stick to the
bottom. Pour the mixture into the bottom of the lined pan and tip the pan
back and forth to spread it out evenly (the mixture will eventually solidify
in the pan, so make sure to spread it out now).

+ Next, spread the pecans (if using) on a baking tray and toast in the oven
for 5 minutes. Remove the pecans from the oven once toasted and set
aside to cool.

+ Now, make the cake batter. Cream together the butter and the sugar in
a large bowl, by hand or with a handheld electric mixer (or freestanding
electric mixer) until it becomes a little lighter in color. Then add the eggs
one at time, beating hard after each addition. Split the vanilla bean
open, scrape the seeds out and add (or add the vanilla extract). Then
fold in both flours, the baking powder, ginger, cinnamon, molasses and
salt and set aside.

+ Take the bananas and slice them into very thin pieces. Arrange them in
a single layer in the bottom of the pan. I line them up so they are nice
and straight, but of course it is fine to do them in any old order too. Pack
them all in tight so they don't move around once the cake mix goes over.
Drizzle over the Calvados, if using.

>

Dulce & banana cake

(continued)

+ Roughly chop the pecans and stir them through the cake batter. Now carefully dollop the cake batter over the bananas and gently spread it out with the back of a spoon or with a palette knife, leveling the top. Then pop it into the oven for 35–45 minutes or so to cook.

+ After the cake has been cooking for 35 minutes, remove it from the oven and insert a metal skewer or the blade of a small knife right into the center (but not touching the bottom). It should come out completely clean. If there is some cakey gooeyness left on it, just pop the pan back in the oven for another 5 minutes or so.

+ Once the cake is baked, remove it from the oven and leave to cool in the pan for about 10 minutes. Then put a large flat plate over the top of the pan and, holding the pan and the plate, flip the whole lot over so that the pan is now upside down. Gently remove the pan and peel off the baking parchment to reveal your very tasty dulce and banana underneath!

+ Cut into squares and serve warm or cold with your choice of crème anglaise, softly whipped cream or ice cream. Salted caramel toffee sauce is also a treat with this (see page 294) or even a store-bought one if you fancy.

Prep time: **25 minutes**
Time baking in the oven:
approximately 25 minutes
Serves: **8**
Equipment: **Kettle, two ¾ x 8-inch
round cake (springform) or tart
pans with removable bottoms,
large baking sheet, mug, 2 large
bowls, pastry brush, wire rack,
fine sieve**

Sponge cake

12 tbsp very soft butter, plus extra for
greasing

1 3 tbsp instant coffee powder

4 oz walnut halves

1 cup self-rising flour

½ cup whole wheat flour

1½ cups soft light brown sugar

1 tsp baking powder

4 medium eggs (at room temperature)

1 tsp vanilla extract

Coffee syrup

1 tsp instant coffee powder

1 tbsp sugar

Buttercream

2¼ cups confectioners' sugar

¾ cup plus 2 tbsp very soft butter

2 tbsp instant coffee powder

Simply coffee, vanilla & walnut cake

One of the first cakes I ever ate was a simple coffee-
flavored cake. No bells, no whistles, nothing fancy,
simply coffee cake with a rich coffee buttercream.
I have, however, played around with the recipe a bit
and added whole wheat flour, which gives a tasty,
nutty dimension to the sponge cake. But if you don't
have whole wheat flour in the cupboard, then just make
this up with all-purpose flour instead for an equally
appetizing cake.

+ Preheat the oven to 350°F, and put the kettle on to boil (with just a small
  amount of water). Grease the bottom of two cake or tart pans with butter
  and line with baking parchment. Set them on a large baking sheet and
  set aside.

+ First make the sponge cake. Put the coffee powder into a mug, using
  1 tablespoon for a subtle coffee flavor or 3 tablespoons if you want
  to be awake for quite some time! For me, 3 is just right. Then add
  1 tablespoon of hot water from the kettle for every tablespoon of coffee
  and mix until smooth. Finely chop half of the walnuts and set aside.

+ Put the flours into a large bowl along with the sugar and baking
  powder and mix a bit to combine. Then add the butter, eggs, vanilla
  extract, prepared coffee and chopped walnuts (reserving the halves for
  decoration). Beat it hard until smooth and well combined. Divide the
  mixture evenly between the two pans and then pop them in the oven for
  around 25 minutes.

+ About 5 minutes before the cake is ready, put the kettle on again for the
  coffee syrup. Spoon the coffee powder into the mug with the sugar and
  2 tablespoons of hot water from the kettle. Stir until the sugar has
  dissolved and set aside.

>

Simply coffee, vanilla & walnut cake

(continued)

+ Check that the cakes are ready. A skewer inserted in the middle should come out clean. Return to the oven for another 5 or so minutes if not. Once ready, remove from the oven and brush liberally with the coffee sugar syrup to give a wonderfully soft sponge. Then leave the cakes for a few minutes until cool enough to handle. Carefully remove from the pans, peel off the paper and leave to cool completely on a wire rack.

+ Cooling should take about 10 minutes. Meanwhile, make the buttercream. Sift the confectioners' sugar into a large bowl. Add the butter and beat hard until light and fluffy. Blend the coffee powder in the mug with 1 tablespoon of hot water from the kettle and stir into the buttercream.

+ Once the cakes have cooled, put one layer on a cake stand or serving plate and slather the top liberally with half of the buttercream. It will be a good thick layer. Place the other cake layer on top and slather the remaining buttercream over. Arrange the remaining walnuts on top. Totally yum.

Prep time: **20 minutes**
Time baking in the oven:
30–40 minutes
Serves: **6 (two slices each)**
Equipment: **Loaf pan, large bowl
and handheld electric mixer
or freestanding electric mixer,
zester, small bowl, wire rack**

½ cup soft butter, plus a little extra for greasing

½ cup sugar

½ vanilla bean (or a couple of drops of vanilla extract)

3 medium eggs (at room temperature)

1 cup self-rising flour

1 tsp baking powder

Pinch of salt

1 lemon

1 lime

4 tbsp poppy seeds

¼ cup confectioners' sugar

Lemon & lime poppy seed drizzle cake

I have made lemon drizzle cake a gazillion times and love it, but I do like to add a twist to recipes. So while tidying up my spice rack, I found a jar of poppy seeds alone in the corner, which had been untouched for some time. I was inspired to throw these into my lemon drizzle mix with some lime for good measure. The resulting cake was a resounding success; the family dived in moments after it surfaced from the oven.

+ Preheat the oven to 350°F, with the middle rack at the ready. Grease and line a loaf pan with baking parchment and grease again. I don't usually line all the sides, but I use a strip that sits in the pan lengthwise and leaves a little overhang at either end. This makes it much easier to pull the cake from the pan once cooked.

+ Cream the butter and sugar together in a large bowl with a handheld electric mixer (or using a freestanding electric mixer) until light and fluffy. Then split open the vanilla bean, scrape out the seeds and add them (or add the vanilla extract) with 2 of the eggs and beat like mad again.

+ The mixture may look less than perfect at this stage, but keep going and it will come out well. Add the last egg and beat like mad, then add the flour, baking powder and salt and finely grate in the lemon and lime zests. Stir the poppy seeds through, then transfer the whole lot into the loaf pan. Spread the mixture flat with the back of a spoon and bake for 35 minutes.

+ Meanwhile, put the confectioners' sugar in a small bowl. Squeeze in about 1 tablespoon of juice from either the lemon or the lime. Add enough to give a runny drizzle, stirring after each addition, and then set this aside.

+ Check the cake after 30 minutes to see if it is done. Insert a skewer or the blade of a small knife into the center of the cake. It should come out clean. If not, pop the cake back into the oven for another 5 minutes or so. Once baked, leave it to cool for a few minutes in the pan. Pull it out using the paper, then peel the parchment off and transfer the cake to a wire rack to cool. Place it on a serving plate, drizzle the drizzle over the top, slice into 12 pieces and serve!

Prep time: **15 minutes, plus 25 minutes to cool and 20 minutes to decorate**
Time baking in the oven: **25–30 minutes**
Serves: **8–10**
Equipment: **Two ¾ x 8-inch round cake (springform) or tart pans with removable bottoms, large baking sheet, large bowl and handheld electric mixer or freestanding electric mixer or food processor, wire rack, medium bowl and microwave or medium saucepan, fine sieve**

Sponge cake

10 tbsp really soft butter, plus a little extra for greasing

¾ cup plus 1 tbsp sugar

1 cup self-rising flour

½ cup sour cream

4 medium eggs (at room temperature)

¼ cup cocoa powder

1 tsp baking powder

Pinch of salt

½ vanilla bean (or a couple of drops of vanilla extract)

Buttercream

4 oz bittersweet or semisweet dark chocolate (minimum 70% cocoa solids)

3 cups confectioners' sugar

1 cup plus 2 tbsp really soft butter

2 tbsp milk (or water)

To decorate

Four 4-oz packages of brown or white Maltesers or malted milk balls

Let them eat cake, cake

The other day my daughter and I were messing around with some M&M's and we stuck them all over a cake. It looked very cool, but was not really very "me." So we both racked our brains and came up with Maltesers as a worthy substitute! This cake is one of those "faster" cakes, rather than "fast," but the all-in-one cake batter is a bung-it-all-in-and-go method, which makes things a lot easier. The great thing that is not quick is sticking on the Malteser balls, but give them to your child (or a willing adult) and let them stick the little balls on to their heart's content.

+ Preheat the oven to 350°F, with the middle rack at the ready. Grease two cake pans with a little butter, line the bottoms with baking parchment and set them on a large baking sheet.

+ Put the butter, sugar, flour, sour cream, eggs, cocoa powder, baking powder and salt in a large bowl or in the bowl of a freestanding electric mixer or a food processor. Split the vanilla bean open, scrape out the seeds and add them also (or the vanilla extract). Then mix or blend to give a smooth, soft mixture.

+ Divide evenly between the cake pans, smooth the tops and place in the oven for 25–30 minutes.

+ To check that the cakes are baked, insert a skewer into the middle of each cake and if it comes out clean, then they are ready to come out. Remove them from the oven and leave to cool in the pans for a few minutes before carefully removing and leaving to cool completely on a wire rack (about 25 minutes).

+ When the cakes are almost cool, start making the buttercream. Break the chocolate into a medium bowl and melt it in the microwave in 30-second blasts, stirring after each blast. Otherwise, set the bowl of chocolate on a medium pan of simmering water, making sure that the water does not touch the bottom of the bowl (as this may make the chocolate grainy).

>

Let them eat cake, cake

(continued)

+ Sift the confectioners' sugar into a large bowl or freestanding electric mixer or processor bowl. If I use a handheld or freestanding electric mixer or processor for this, I don't worry about sifting it as the blade will do a good job of blending in any lumps. Add the butter and milk (or water) and beat until it is really light and fluffy. You will need to do this like mad if blending by hand. Then pour in the melted chocolate, stirring all the time.

+ Set one of the cakes on a serving plate or cake stand. I often put a little dollop of buttercream underneath the layer so that the cake does not move around. Then put about a third of the buttercream on and spread it around. Then set the other layer on top and spread the remaining buttercream all over so it is completely covered. It doesn't need to be perfect. Doing this is a great excuse to get nice and messy.

+ Once you have covered the cake, and of course yourself, suitably in chocolate, take the Maltesers or malted milk balls and stick them all over the cake. I am pedantic about this as I want the malt balls to be in strict rows, so I start at the base of the cake and then go in a line, up the side, over the top and down the other side. I am not ashamed to say that rulers have been used in the decorating of this cake for a supersharp line! Line them up nice and tight with no gaps.

+ Once the cake is covered, carry to the table and serve.

Prep time: 25 minutes
Time baking in the oven:
35–40 minutes
Makes: 6 wedges
Equipment: 9-inch springform
pan, large baking sheet, large
bowl, 3 medium bowls, fine sieve,
zester, wire rack

1 cup sunflower (or other flavorless)
oil, plus extra for greasing

¾ cup plus 1 tbsp sugar

½ cup low-fat milk

4 medium eggs (at room temperature)

A few drops of vanilla extract

2 cups self-rising flour

1 tsp baking powder

2 tbsp cocoa powder

1 orange

Crouching tiger, hidden zebra cake

The cake of many stripes. Another mad scientist moment. I had a red velvet cheesecake, Stateside, which looks very similar to this cake. I asked the proprietors of the café, but they were keeping mum on how they created their "target" cake. So it was into the kitchen for a day of cakey fun and frolics to reproduce the look.

+ Preheat the oven to 350°F. Grease the bottom of a springform pan with a little oil, line with baking parchment and oil again. Set aside on a large baking sheet.

+ Put the oil, sugar, milk, eggs and vanilla extract in a large bowl and beat everything together well. It is best not to use an electric mixer as it will introduce too many bubbles, which are not needed for this cake.

+ Pour 1½ cups of this mixture into a medium bowl.

+ Sift 1 cup plus 2 tbsp of the self-rising flour into one bowl along with ½ teaspoon of the baking powder. Mix well and set aside. This is your vanilla mix.

+ Sift the remaining flour and ½ teaspoon of baking powder into the other bowl along with the cocoa powder. Finely grate the orange zest in, mix everything together well and set aside. This is your chocolate batter.

+ Now, put a tablespoon of the vanilla batter in the middle of the pan. Then, using a clean tablespoon, put a blob of the chocolate batter in the middle of the vanilla one. Keep doing this, alternating between vanilla and chocolate, so you form a type of "bull's eye" or "target board" look. Each time you dollop a blob in, the whole mix will spread out on the base. By the time you have used up both of the cake mixes, the batter should have just reached the edge of the pan.

+ Bake in the oven for 35 minutes.

>

Crouching tiger, hidden zebra cake

(continued)

+ Check that the cake is baked by inserting a skewer into the center. It should come out clean. If not, then return to the oven for another 5 minutes or so until cooked. Once cooked, remove from the oven and allow to cool for a few minutes in the pan. Then carefully remove from the pan and leave to cool completely on a wire rack (but it is also fine to eat it warm!).

+ Cut the cake into six wedges to reveal its spongy gold. Arrange on a cake stand or platter and serve.

Bread + pastry

Food for the body is not enough.
There must be food for the soul as well.
Dorothy Day

I am truly, madly, deeply passionate about bread.
I don't just mean I am in love with eating the entire
bread basket every time I go out for a meal, with
lashings of the butter that accompanies it; I mean the
making of it. There are days when I feel on top of the
world and days when the world feels like it has all its
weight on me, but often I will throw some flour and the
other necessary ingredients into a bowl and use the
making of the dough as a mode of therapy to get me
out of my black dog blues. Kneading by hand releases
a multitude of angst and the smell of freshly baked
bread fills my head with happiness. Fresh home-baked
bread is instant culinary gratification at its finest.

Prep time: **15 minutes**

Time baking in the oven:
35 minutes

Makes: **1 loaf**

Equipment: **Baking tray, large bowl**

---

3 sprigs of fresh rosemary

3 oz (⅓ cup) pitted green or black olives

3¼ cups self-rising flour, plus extra for dusting

½ tsp salt

1 tbsp extra virgin olive oil

¾ cup cold water

Fruity olive oil and balsamic vinegar

Aussie olive damper bread (soda bread's antipodean cousin)

I first went to Sydney in my teens and when I saw the Opera House, I fell head over heels in love with the place. This is an Australian bread traditionally (I am led to believe) made by people in the bush on the campfire. I love green olives, but the black variety, although normally a little more bitter, work well too.

+ Preheat the oven to 400°F and put a baking tray in to warm up.

+ Pick the leaves from the rosemary and roughly chop them up. Roughly chop the olives also, and set both aside in separate piles.

+ Put the flour in a large bowl with the rosemary, salt, oil and water. Mix everything well until the dough starts to come together in a ball. Then get your hands in and squeeze in all the dry bits, using the dough like a cloth to gather all the bits up.

+ Dust a clean work surface with a little flour and place the dough down. Press it into a flattish round, put the olives in the center and squash them down a bit, bringing the edges of the dough toward the center to cover the olives. Flip the dough over and knead the olives in. The dough may be quite wet with olives flying all around, but just keep pushing the rogue olives back into the dough. If everything is too wet, add a small handful of flour. Shape the dough into an 8-inch round and place on the warmed baking tray.

+ Rub a little flour onto the handle of a wooden spoon. Then, holding the handle horizontal to the bread, press down on the loaf, making an indent almost to the bottom of the tray. Now turn the handle so that it is at a 90-degree angle to the first line and push down again to make a cross. Do this two more times so your bread looks like a kind of clock face of eight triangular portions.

+ Bake in the oven for 35 minutes or until the bread sounds hollow when tapped on the bottom. This is wonderful served warm with some fruity olive oil and balsamic vinegar.

Prep time: **10 minutes**
Proofing time: **30–45 minutes**
Time baking in the oven:
25 minutes
Makes: **1 loaf**
Equipment: **Large bowl or freestanding electric mixer set with the dough hook, baking sheet, small bowl**

Bread

2¾ cups white bread flour, plus extra for dusting

⅓ cup whole wheat bread flour

¼-oz package of fast-acting dried yeast

2 tsp salt

1 cup water

A little sunflower oil (or oil spray)

Topping

¼ cup rice flour (I found rice flour online from most supermarkets)

1 tsp sugar

¼ tsp fast-acting dried yeast

Pinch of salt

1 tsp vegetable oil

1 tbsp warm water

Crackle-top bread

This is one of my cheeky recipes that I have slipped into the book under the guise of its being fast(er) to prepare compared to using regular yeast, and because there is also very little work to do. So a bit of slow stirring and kneading and that is basically it. Now, this little bread has caused some controversy recently over whether it looks like a giraffe or the tiger after which it is usually named, but for me, I prefer the U.S. name "Dutch crunch" or my own made-up name, crackle-top bread.

+ First, prepare the bread. Put the flours, yeast and salt into a large bowl (or freestanding electric mixer) and give a quick mix to combine. Add 1 cup of water, mixing all the time until everything comes together. Then get your hands in and squidge it into a ball. Add a couple more tablespoons of water if it's too dry. Knead it on a floured work surface for 10 minutes (or 5 minutes if using a freestanding electric mixer).

+ To check that the dough has been kneaded enough, first make it into a ball with a taut top. Then dip your finger in some flour and prod the side of the dough to make an indent. If the dough springs back all the way, it is ready. If it only springs back a little, knead it for a couple more minutes and try again.

+ Now flatten the bread ball out a little (to give a loaf roughly 2 inches high by 4½ inches wide). Then pull the edges into the middle, making a little parcel-type thing, and turn it over. This will give the dough a nice taut top. Cup the edges of the dough with your hands to shape it into a neat round shape and place on a baking sheet.

+ Oil some plastic wrap and wrap it over the dough. Use several pieces if necessary so that the dough is completely covered, but not too tightly so that there is room to rise. Put in a warm (but not too hot) place for 30–45 minutes or until it has increased in size by about 50 percent.

+ Preheat the oven to 400°F, with the top rack at the ready.

>

Crackle-top bread

(continued)

+ Next, prepare the topping. Mix the rice flour in a small bowl with the sugar, yeast and salt. Add the oil and warm water and stir into a thickish paste. Cover and set aside in a warm area until ready to use.

+ To check that the dough is risen enough, remove the plastic wrap, dip your finger in some flour and then dip it into the side of the bread, making a small indent. If the dough springs back halfway, it is ready.

+ Once the dough has sufficiently proofed, use your hands to rub the topping paste all over the top and sides in a nice even layer. Then put the dough in the oven for 25 minutes.

+ The bread should be crackled on top; if not, pop it back in the oven until it starts to darken. If it is crackled, give the bread a tap underneath. It should sound hollow, but if it is not quite there yet, put it back in the oven for another 5 minutes or so. Once ready, remove it from the oven and allow to cool a bit. This is best served with lashings of butter.

Prep time: **25 minutes**
Chilling-out time (aka proofing
time): **30 minutes**
More chilling-out time (aka time
baking in the oven): **35–40 minutes**
Makes: **1 loaf**
Equipment: **Large bowl or
freestanding electric mixer
set with the dough hook, rolling
pin, pastry brush, baking sheet**

4¼ cups white bread flour, plus extra
for dusting

¾ cup whole wheat bread flour

2 tsp salt

¼-oz package of fast-acting dried
yeast

2 squeezes or dabs of honey

1½ cups warm water (from the tap)

1 tbsp sesame oil

2 oz (¼ cup) poppy seeds

Sunflower oil or spray oil

Twister bread

This very fine "tear and share" bread will take only
25 minutes of your "active" time to make. The rest of the
time you can be emailing, dancing or watching TV.
I really love the flavors and the textures of this bread,
with its crispy crunchy outside and the soft and chewy
inside. Mix things up if you fancy a different filling—
substitute sundried tomatoes or tapenade for the poppy
seeds. Or go really mad with some Nutella and toasted
hazelnuts for a sweet, chocolatey filling.

+ Put the flours, salt and yeast into a large bowl (or freestanding electric
  mixer), mix a bit and then make a hole in the middle. Mix in the
  honey and add in 1½ cups of warm water (from the tap). Then mix
  everything together until combined. I like to get my hands in (I find it very
  therapeutic!) and press it all together, gathering up all those dry bits from
  the bottom of the bowl.

+ Turn the dough out onto a floured work surface and knead it for
  10 minutes (or 5 minutes if kneading in a freestanding electric mixer).
  To test and see if it has been kneaded enough, form the dough into a
  ball with a nice taut top. Dip your finger in the flour and then prod the
  side of the dough, making an indent. The indent should spring back all
  the way and almost disappear if the dough is ready.

+ Put some more flour on the work surface and then, using a rolling pin, roll
  the dough out into a rectangle about 16 x 9 inches. If it is too springy to
  roll, then cover it with a clean tea towel and leave for 5 minutes or so.
  That way the stretchy gluten strands in the bread can relax a bit, which
  will make it easier to roll out.

+ Using a pastry brush, brush the top of the dough with the sesame oil,
  going right up to the edges, and sprinkle the poppy seeds evenly all over.
  Cut the dough into six 1¾-inch-wide strips down the length.

+ Keeping the strips lined up together, twist each one up like a twisted
  breadstick or cheese straw. Once they are all twisted, stack them into

>

Twister bread

(continued)

a bundle and pick them all up in one go. Then twist them together so you have a long, thick twisted rope made up of the individual strands of bread. Try to twist it so the rope maintains an even thickness throughout.

+ Now curve the bread into a wreath shape and press the ends together, sealing them with a bit of water. It does not have to be perfect, just as long as the ends are joined up. When I make this bread there are usually lots of poppy seeds left on the surface, so I scoop these up and scatter them over the bread, especially where the join is, to cover it up a bit.

+ Place the wreath on a baking sheet. Oil some plastic wrap (I find the spray oil is best for this) and use it to cover the dough, oiled side down, so it is airtight but with enough room for the dough to rise a little.

+ I usually put the oven to preheat to 400°F now and place the dough on a chair near it, so it's nice and warm. Leave to proof for about 30 minutes. To test if it is ready for the oven (because the bread will not have doubled in size, but probably grown by about half again), dust your finger with some flour and then make an indent in the side of the bread. The indent should spring back about halfway. If the indent just stays there and does not really move very much, then the dough needs more time.

+ When ready, place in the oven to bake for 35 minutes.

+ The loaf is cooked when it sounds hollow when tapped underneath. If not, then give it another 5 minutes or so in the oven.

+ Once ready, remove from the oven and serve. I love the crispy crunchy bits on the outside and the soft pillowy inside slathered in lots of butter.

Net bread (roti jala)

Time from start to finish:
20 minutes
Makes: **6 rotis**
Equipment: **Deep bowl, large frying pan (at least 12 inches wide), piping bag fitted with a very small nozzle or a disposable piping bag or squeeze bottle, baking tray**

1 cup all-purpose flour
2 tsp curry powder
Pinch of salt
¾ cup coconut milk
1 medium egg
Vegetable oil

This Malaysian-inspired "roti" looks suspiciously like my dear nan's favorite crocheted doily. I find the combination of coconut milk and curry powder a little bit addictive and make these to accompany anything a bit spicy with lots of sauce. Just fold up the rotis and mop up the juices. They're also delicious with some homemade mango chutney (see page 293). Very, very tasty.

+ Preheat the oven to 225°F.

+ Put the flour, curry powder and salt into a deep bowl and make a well in the center. Gradually add the coconut milk, stirring all the time. Once all of the coconut milk is added, beat it hard to get rid of any lumps. Then crack the egg in, beat again and set aside.

+ Pour a tiny bit of oil into a large frying pan on a medium to high heat.

+ Pour the mixture into the piping bag fitted with a very narrow nozzle, or if you are using a disposable piping bag, simply snip enough from the tip of the bag to make a very small hole. As the mixture is fairly runny, you will need to press the nozzle opening of the bag closed so it doesn't flow out as you fill it. Alternatively, you can use a squeeze bottle for this. You may need to snip a little off the bottle tip to make the opening ever so slightly bigger. It's a bit messy filling it up, but will still produce lovely rotis!

+ Once the pan is nice and hot, drizzle the mixture onto it in a loop-the-loop pattern, up and down the pan until all is covered. Make sure that all of the rows join up together so that the "net" will hold once it is cooked.

+ Leave to cook for about 3 minutes or until the underside is just beginning to go a golden brown. Then carefully flip it over (as you would a pancake) and cook the other side for a couple of minutes.

+ Once the bread is cooked, slide it out of the pan onto a baking tray. Place in the oven to keep warm while you make the remaining five rotis in the same way. Layer sheets of baking parchment between them as you go to prevent them sticking together.

+ Serve at once.

Puff pastry

Prep time: **30 minutes**
Chilling time in the fridge: **1 hour
55 minutes**
Makes: **1¼ pounds**
Equipment: **Large bowl, rolling
pin, pastry brush, baking tray**

2 cups all-purpose flour, plus extra for
dusting
½ tsp salt
3 tbsp cold butter, cubed
½ cup cold water
¾ cup plus 2 tbsp soft butter (see
headnote)

The block of butter in this recipe is divided into two parts—the smaller bit should be chilled and the rest needs to be nice and soft. The best way to get the right softness and shape is to put the butter between two sheets of wax paper or baking parchment and bash it with a rolling pin until pliable.

+ Put the flour, salt and chilled butter into a large bowl and rub them together with your fingertips until they resemble fine breadcrumbs. Make a well in the center of the mixture and pour in ½ cup of cold water. Mix with a knife, then bring the dough together with your hands.

+ Press into a ball, then wrap in plastic wrap and put in the freezer for 15 minutes (or in the fridge for 25 minutes).

+ Unwrap the dough ball and use a knife to score a large cross in the middle of it, cutting no more than halfway through. Lift all four corners from the middle of the cross, then pull them up and out to make the cross big enough to put the softened butter into.

+ Add the butter, then fold the corners of the cross back to the center, covering the butter so it is completely enclosed. The corners should overlap in the center so no butter is showing. It is important that the butter is not too hard or too soft, otherwise it will escape through the dough when you roll it out and the resulting pastry will not rise as well. If it's too hard, leave the ball of pastry at room temperature until the butter inside has softened; if it is getting too soft, pop it in the freezer for 10 minutes (or in the fridge for 20 minutes) to firm up a little before rolling.

+ This next process is called "rolling and folding" (or "turns") and it creates the characteristic flaky layers of puff pastry. Begin by rolling the pastry out away from you on a well-floured work surface into a rectangle roughly three times as long as it is wide (don't turn the pastry when rolling). Keep the corners square and edges straight by pressing a palette knife or ruler against them. Lift the dough occasionally to make sure it isn't sticking; flour the work surface again if necessary and sprinkle with more flour as you go, dusting away any excess with a pastry brush. Take the

>

Puff pastry

(continued)

short edge of the pastry nearest to you and fold it up a third, then fold the top edge down a third to give a rectangular block. Turn the dough 90 degrees and then repeat the rolling and folding.

+ You have now given the dough two "rolls and folds." Wrap the dough in plastic wrap and chill in the fridge for 20 minutes.

+ Remove the dough from the fridge, unwrap and give it two more "rolls and folds." Wrap and rest in the fridge for at least another 20 minutes. The block of puff pastry can at this point be kept in the fridge for a day or two, or frozen.

+ Remove from the fridge, unwrap and give the dough a final couple of rolls and folds, then roll it out to the size desired for your chosen recipe. Place on a baking tray, cover with oiled plastic wrap and leave to rest in the fridge for about 30 minutes before using.

Prep time: **5 minutes or 10 minutes if making by hand**
Chilling time in the fridge:
30 minutes
Makes: **1 pound**
Equipment: **Food processor or medium bowl**

2 cups all-purpose flour

½ cup soft butter

2 tbsp soft light brown sugar

Pinch of salt

1 egg

Sweet rich brown sugar pastry

A warm, toasty flavored pastry, made in the food processor in 5 minutes. This is a great base for sweet tarts and flans. If the pastry becomes too soft when you are rolling it out, then just pop it in the freezer for 5 minutes to firm up.

+ Put the flour, butter, sugar and salt in a food processor and blend until the mixture resembles fine breadcrumbs. Then add the egg and blitz for a minute or so more until the mix looks like it is just coming together.

+ Remove the processor blade and get your hands into the mixture, bringing it together into a ball.

+ If you are making the pastry by hand, then mix the butter, sugar and salt together in a bowl until combined. Add the egg and stir until mixed in, then add the flour and mix it through with as few stirs as possible.

+ Then wrap the pastry in plastic wrap and place it in the fridge for 30 minutes to firm up.

+ Use as required (or keep in the freezer, defrosting for use at a later stage).

Prep time: **5 minutes or 10 minutes if making by hand**
Chilling time in the fridge:
30 minutes
Makes: **1 pound**
Equipment: **Food processor or medium bowl**

2 cups all-purpose flour

½ cup cold butter

2 tbsp confectioners' sugar

Pinch of salt

2 medium egg yolks

Sweet shortcrust pastry

This is an easy-peasy pastry that is made in the food processor in a matter of minutes. The shops do have great ready-made versions too, which in truth are often easier to handle as they are not rich with butter and so not as crumbly as homemade. But nothing can beat the taste of one made from scratch. And as you roll it out, if it does break up, just patch it back together. Should the pastry become too soft, then pop it into the freezer for a couple of minutes to give the butter a chance to firm up a little, making for manageable rolling out.

+ Blitz the flour, butter, sugar and salt in a food processor. Add the egg yolks and blitz a bit more until the dough forms a ball. If the dough is still a bit dry, just add a tablespoon of cold water and mix a bit more.

+ If you are making the pastry by hand, put the flour and butter in a medium bowl then pick up bits of the flour and butter and rub them together, letting the mixture fall back into the bowl. Keep lifting up bits of butter and flour (up nice and high so more air gets into them and they stay nice and cool) until the mixture resembles breadcrumbs. Then stir in the sugar and salt. Next add the egg yolks, mixing them in well with a spoon until it all comes together. If the dough is still feeling a bit dry, add a tablespoon of cold water to help bring it together.

+ Put the pastry onto a lightly floured work surface. Knead into a smooth ball, wrap in plastic wrap and rest in the fridge for 30 minutes until firm. Then use as required.

Tasty treats

Anything is good if it's made of chocolate.
Jo Brand

I had all sorts of recipe odds and ends that I wasn't quite sure where to put—those tasty little things such as tarts and muffins and easy bars that form so much of my weekend cooking. As my friends and family can attest, I am often in the kitchen with a whole load of ingredients, throwing stuff together in a bid to conjure up some magical, tasty spell. During these times, my hair is usually gray from confectioners' sugar and there is a smudge of white chocolate on my chin, but I am always sporting my gapped-tooth grin with various sweet treats and other tasty morsels balancing on trays and plates around my kitchen, many of which can be found here.

Little jammy tarts

Prep time: **15 minutes**
Time baking in the oven:
20–25 minutes
Makes: **12 tarts**
Equipment: **12-cup muffin pan,
rolling pin, 3-inch round cutter,
2-inch star cutter, mug or small
bowl, pastry brush, wire rack**

A little sunflower oil or oil spray,
for greasing

A handful of all-purpose flour

1-lb package of sweet shortcrust pastry
(or you can make my sweet rich brown
sugar pastry on page 268)

12 tbsp of either one type or a
selection of preserves, such as lemon
curd, blackberry, strawberry or
raspberry jam

1 medium egg

Cutting culinary corners is a huge blessing for me at times and pastry is often not the easiest of things for lots of people to make. In actual fact, I often encourage people who are starting out with cooking to experiment initially with store-bought pastry as a way of getting used to it before embarking on making their own. These little jammy tarts evoke happy memories from my youth and eating them while still warm from the oven offers me comfort, warmth and calm.

+ Preheat the oven to 350°F. Lightly grease a 12-cup muffin pan with oil (an oil spray is handy for this) and set aside.

+ Using a rolling pin, roll the pastry out on a lightly floured work surface to about ¼ inch thick. Then, using the round cutter and the star cutter, stamp out 12 of each shape. Reroll the pastry as necessary to use it all up.

+ Line each cup of the muffin pan with a pastry disk, very gently pushing them down. Prick a few holes in the bottom of the pastry with a fork so that it does not puff up when baking. Then spoon a tablespoon of your choice of preserve into each one before sitting a pastry star on top.

+ Crack the egg into a mug or small bowl, whisk lightly with a fork and then brush each star with the egg.

+ Place the pan in the freezer for 5 minutes to harden up the tarts a bit so that the butter does not melt before the flour has had a chance to harden (which would leave the tarts in a soggy mess. Anyway, that is not going to happen here.).

+ Remove from the freezer and bake for 20–25 minutes.

+ Once cooked, the pastry should be crisp and golden brown. Leave to cool in the pan for a few minutes before carefully removing onto a wire rack to cool completely. These are delicious eaten slightly warm, but be careful not to burn yourself with potentially piping-hot jam.

Prep time: 25 minutes
Chilling time: 30 minutes in the
freezer or 1 hour in the fridge
Makes: 16 squares
Equipment: 8-inch square cake
pan, large saucepan, small
bowl and microwave or small
saucepan, blender or food
processor

½ cup plus 2 tbsp butter

7 oz bittersweet or semisweet
chocolate (minimum 70% cocoa solids)
or milk chocolate, or a mixture of both

9 oz digestive biscuits or graham
crackers

¾ cup soft light brown sugar

11 oz (1⅓ cups) crunchy peanut butter

1 tsp vanilla extract

Peanut butter squares

I was recipe-testing some millionaire's shortbread and found I did not have enough of the correct ingredients. A family-sized jar of crunchy peanut butter sat almost full at the back of my cupboard, providing me with some nutty inspiration for these peanut butter squares.

+ Line a cake pan with baking parchment, leaving some excess paper hanging over the edges (this makes it easier to lift out the squares once set).

+ Put the butter in a large saucepan and leave to melt slowly on a low heat.

+ Snap the chocolate into squares and throw into a small bowl. Then melt in the microwave in 30-second blasts, stirring well after each blast. Alternatively, set the bowl over a pan of simmering water. Make sure that the bottom of the bowl does not touch the water or the chocolate may seize and go really grainy and stiff.

+ Remove the butter from the heat once melted.

+ Blitz the digestive biscuits or graham crackers and brown sugar in a blender or food processor to give fine crumbs. Add to the butter, scoop in the peanut butter and vanilla extract and mix together well so everything is combined.

+ Put the mixture in the lined pan and press it down really hard with the back of a spoon. It needs to be really compact and tight. Then pour over the melted chocolate, tilting the pan back and forth a bit so that the whole thing is evenly covered. Pop in the freezer for 30 minutes to firm up (or in the fridge for 1 hour).

+ Once the chocolate is set, remove it from the freezer (or fridge). Lift it out of the pan with the help of the baking parchment. Remove the paper and then use a sharp knife to divide it into 16 squares to serve. These will last for a few days in an airtight container.

Vanilla hazelnut & brown sugar shortbread

Prep time: **15 minutes**
Chilling time: **15 minutes in the freezer or 30 minutes in the fridge**
Time baking in the oven:
25 minutes
Cooling time: **About 25 minutes**
Makes: **8 wedges**
Equipment: **Medium bowl, 8-inch round springform pan, wire rack**

¾ cup plus 2 tbsp soft butter

½ cup soft light brown sugar

½ vanilla bean (or a few drops of vanilla extract)

2 oz (¼ cup) roasted chopped hazelnuts (they come ready roasted and chopped from most supermarkets)

2 cups plus 1 tbsp all-purpose flour

1 egg yolk

Sugar, for dusting

The inclusion of soft light brown sugar in this recipe in place of the more common white sugar adds a warm, caramelized taste to the shortbread and deepens its flavor. Hazelnuts add a nutty note, but these can be replaced by any toasted nut of your choice. Try chopping up a little fresh ginger and adding that to the mix for a spicy variation too.

+ Put the butter in a medium bowl with the soft light brown sugar and beat together to combine.

+ Split the vanilla bean, scrape out the seeds and add them (or the vanilla extract) to the mixture along with the hazelnuts, flour and egg yolk and mix everything together well. It is kind of a crumbly mixture, so I find the best way to mix it together is to squash everything on the side of the bowl with the back of a wooden spoon.

+ Pour the mixture into the springform pan. Then I like to get my hands in and squish it all out into a nice flat layer, finishing it off with the back of a spoon to get it really smooth.

+ Now decorate around the edge of the shortbread. Nothing fancy needed here; I just put a little flour on the tips of my index and middle fingers and press them down all the way around the edge of the shortbread to give a nice "crimped" pattern. Use a knife to lightly mark out eight wedges and use a fork to prick each one three times, to give the shortbread the trademark look.

+ Put the mixture in the freezer for 15 minutes to firm up (or in the fridge for 30 minutes). Preheat the oven to 350°F.

+ Once the oven is ready, bake the shortbread for 25 minutes.

+ The shortbread should be just firm and a very light golden color. Once cooked, remove from the oven and dust with the sugar. Allow it to cool in the pan for a few minutes before carefully removing and leaving to cool completely on a wire rack. Then cut it into wedges along the marked-out lines and enjoy. It will keep for a few days in an airtight container.

Prep time: 15 minutes
Time baking in the oven:
25–30 minutes
Makes: 12 muffins
Equipment: Small saucepan,
12-cup muffin pan, paper liners
(or baking parchment and
scissors), large bowl

½ cup butter

2 cups plus 2 tbsp self-rising flour

1¾ cups soft light brown sugar
(granulated sugar will also work)

3 oz (6 tbsp) rolled oats

1 tsp baking powder

1 tsp baking soda

Pinch of salt

7 oz fresh or frozen blueberries

11 oz (1⅓ cups) sour cream

2 medium eggs

1 medium egg yolk

Blueberry & oat muffins

These are my daughter's absolute favorites. I make a huge batch on a Sunday night and she takes them to school to eat at break time during the week. I use sour cream in the recipe, which gives the finished product a wonderful light texture compared to using milk. The trick to a light and fluffy muffin is not to stir the batter too much, but either way these will still taste good.

+ Preheat the oven to 350°F, with the middle rack at the ready.

+ Put the butter into a small saucepan over a low heat and leave to melt.

+ Line a 12-cup muffin pan with paper liners or cut out 9 x 6-inch squares from the baking parchment. Take two squares and place one on top of the other like a star, then push them down into the muffin cups and repeat until all the cups are lined. They may pop up a bit but once the batter is in, they will stay down!

+ Remove the butter from the heat and leave to cool.

+ Put the flour, sugar, 4 tbsp of the oats, the baking powder, baking soda and salt into a large bowl, mix together and then make a hole in the center.

+ Put two-thirds of the blueberries into the hole, dollop in the sour cream, add the eggs and egg yolk, pour in the cooled melted butter and stir everything gently to just combine. Divide the batter between the 12 cups. The batter will give just enough to fill each one right to the top.

+ Press the remaining blueberries lightly into the tops and then sprinkle the remaining oats evenly over.

+ Bake in the oven for 25–30 minutes or until a skewer inserted into the center of the muffins comes out clean (try not to hit any blueberries or the skewer will not come out clean). The muffins should also be springy to the touch and golden brown.

+ Eat warm or cold. These will keep for a few days in an airtight container or they freeze well also.

Prep time: 10 minutes
Time baking in the oven:
15 minutes
Makes: About 2¾ pounds
Equipment: 2 large roasting
pans, large bowl

½ cup maple syrup

2 tbsp sugar

2 tbsp sunflower oil

½ tsp vanilla extract

2 cups rolled oats

6 oz (¾ cup) mixed seeds (such as pumpkin, sunflower, sesame or flaxseeds)

5 oz pecans (or walnuts)

2 oz whole almonds

1 oz flaked almonds

3 oz desiccated coconut

Pinch of salt (optional)

2 tsp ground cinnamon (optional)

5 oz dried cranberries

Maple, pecan & cranberry granola

Nutty, fruity wholesome goodness—a must for the oat lover's kitchen repertoire. Please feel free to ad lib here, with substitutions such as honey for the maple syrup, raisins, apricots or dried apples for the dried cranberries and cashews for the whole almonds.

+ Preheat the oven to 325°F. Line two large roasting pans with baking parchment and set aside.

+ Put the maple syrup, sugar, oil and vanilla extract into a large bowl and mix well. Then toss in the oats, mixed seeds, pecans (or walnuts), whole almonds, flaked almonds, coconut and salt and cinnamon, if using. Give the mixture a good stir and then get your hands in, picking it up and letting it fall down to coat and moisten everything really well.

+ Pour the mixture into the roasting pans and spread it out evenly. Bake in the oven for about 15 minutes, giving it a good stir and swapping the pans on their racks halfway through.

+ The granola should be golden when cooked. Remove and leave to cool completely before stirring the cranberries in. Store in an airtight container for up to a month.

Time from start to finish:
15 minutes
(plus overnight preserving)
Makes: About 2 pounds or
enough to fill a 3-cup jar
Equipment: 3¼-cup Ball or jam
jar (with lid), small saucepan,
zester, colander

1⅔ cups soft light brown sugar

⅔ cup port

1 tsp ground cinnamon

1 orange

⅔ cup water

12 oz fresh cherries

Port-preserved cherries with cinnamon & orange

These are delicious nibbled on straight from the jar or served warm or at room temperature with anything chocolatey or creamy. The pits are still in the cherries, so it might be best to warn people of this first!

+ Sterilize a Ball or jam jar (and its lid) in the dishwasher on the hottest setting or carefully put them in just-boiled water (off the heat) for a couple of minutes and dry with a clean towel.

+ Put the sugar, port and cinnamon in a small saucepan and finely grate the orange zest in. Halve and juice the orange, adding the juice with ⅔ cup of water.

+ Then bring everything slowly to the boil, stirring every so often until the sugar dissolves. Let it boil away for 3 minutes until thick and syrupy and then remove and leave to cool.

+ Meanwhile, wash the cherries in a colander and remove their stems if desired, but I think they look great left on. Place them in the sterilized jar.

+ Once cooled, pour the syrup over the cherries, seal the jar and leave to sit at least overnight. The cherries will last for a week if kept nice and airtight in the jar.

Prep time: **15 minutes**
Chilling time: **15 minutes**
Makes: **About 40**
Equipment: **Large tray or
baking sheet, medium bowl and
microwave or medium saucepan,
colander**

---

4 oz white chocolate

1 lb cherries (preferably with stems still attached)

White chocolate–dipped cherries

I was driving around northern Spain last year and was taken aback by the many, many cherries for sale by the roadside. Big fat cherries bursting with juice and as shiny as a mirror. But after my third bag, I felt they needed a bit of variation. Having found a jumbo bar of white chocolate in the fridge, this "recipe" was born. If you fancy it, after dipping the cherries in the white chocolate, dip them in some ground-up nuts for a bit of variation.

+ Line a large tray or baking sheet with baking parchment and then set this aside.

+ Break the chocolate into a medium bowl. I like to melt chocolate in a microwave in 30-second blasts, stirring after each blast. Alternatively, melt the chocolate in a bowl that just sits on top of a medium saucepan with a little bit of boiling water. Make sure the bowl doesn't touch the water as this could make the chocolate grainy.

+ White chocolate is more difficult to melt than dark or milk. There is a fine line between its being just melted and its burning and drying out (where it becomes thick and "doughy"). Keep a close eye on it and as soon as it starts melting, stir for a few seconds and then remove from the heat.

+ Wash the cherries in a colander and pat dry with paper towels. Then, holding a cherry by the stem, dip it halfway into the melted chocolate. I like to dip them at a slight angle as I think it looks a bit cooler. Then shake off the excess and set the cherry, stem side up, on the tray or baking sheet. Repeat with the rest of the cherries.

+ Place the coated cherries in the fridge for at least 15 minutes, or until the chocolate hardens, before serving. I think these look so pretty when presented all together on a big plate or cake stand.

Prep time: 10 minutes for disk lollipops or 20 minutes for trellis-type
Chilling time: 15 minutes
Makes: About 10 lollipops
Equipment: Large tray or baking sheet, 10 lollipop sticks, medium bowl and medium pan or microwave, scissors and transparent tape or stapler (optional)

4 oz white chocolate

1 tbsp dried cranberries

White chocolate lollipops with dried cranberries

The best chocolate for these lollipops is cheap white children's chocolate. You can use sprinkles, nuts or dried fruits other than cranberries for these; just about anything that does not have too much moisture content will work.

+ Line a large tray or baking sheet with baking parchment so the paper is really flat (making sure that the tray will fit in the fridge a bit later on). Lay the lollipop sticks out on the sheet, spaced well apart.

+ Snap the chocolate up a bit into a medium bowl and either melt in the microwave in 30-second blasts, stirring after each blast, or set over a pan of simmering water, making sure that the bottom of the bowl does not touch the water.

+ White chocolate is more difficult to melt than dark or milk. There is a fine line between its being just melted and its burning and drying out (where it becomes thick and "doughy"). Keep a close eye on it and as soon as it starts melting, stir for a few seconds and then remove from the heat.

+ If making disk lollipops, simply place a spoonful of melted chocolate on top of one end of each of the sticks to give a 1¾-inch disk. If making trellis-type lollipops, cut out a 5-inch square of baking parchment, then roll it into a cone shape and gently pull the flap on the inside to tighten the whole thing and create a nozzle tip. Secure down the side with some tape or a stapler, then snip the tip with scissors to give a very narrow nozzle opening. Spoon the melted chocolate in and fold down the top of the piping bag so the chocolate does not squidge out the wrong end.

+ Gently squeeze the chocolate from the piping bag to draw whatever shape you like over one end of each of the sticks. Flick it over and back in a crisscross pattern or go around and around in circles, for example.

+ Once your chosen lollipop shapes have been made, finely chop the cranberries and scatter them over the chocolate to stick.

+ Place them in the fridge for at least 15 minutes or until set. Very carefully peel the lollipops off the paper and serve. They will keep for up to a month in the fridge (if they have survived not being eaten!).

Prep time: 10 minutes
Chilling time: 25 minutes in the
freezer or 50 minutes in the
fridge
Coating time: 10–15 minutes
(depending on which finish you
go for)
Makes: 18–20 lollipops
Equipment: Large baking tray,
food processor (or plastic
food bag, rolling pin and
medium bowl), 18–20 6-inch
(approximately) lollipop sticks
(the white rounded type), small
bowl and microwave or small
pan, small bowls

Lollipops

Two 5-oz packages of Oreo cookies

5 oz cream cheese (or chocolate
cream cheese or Nutella)

Coating

7 oz white chocolate (the cheapest you
can find)

2 tsp (per lollipop) of hundreds and
thousands (nonpareils) or chopped
nuts (optional)

Shameless shortcut cookies-and-cream lollipops

White chocolate is a curious beast as it is not really chocolate, containing no actual cocoa solids whatsoever. Because of this, it tends to go lumpy and thick more quickly than our darker chocolate friends. So if you find when using it that it becomes gloopy, just melt it again and it should be fine. The lollipops can be dipped in hundreds and thousands (nonpareils) or chopped nuts after being dipped in the white chocolate if you fancy it.

+ Line a large baking tray (that will fit in your freezer or fridge) with baking parchment and set aside.

+ Put the Oreos in a food processor and whiz them up to fine crumbs. Then add the cream cheese (or chocolate cream cheese or Nutella) and whiz until the mixture starts to form a ball.

+ If you are not using a food processor, pop the cookies in a plastic bag and bash them to fine crumbs with a rolling pin. Transfer them to a medium bowl and stir in the cream cheese (or chocolate cream cheese or Nutella) until the mixture begins to stick together.

+ With cold hands, roll the mixture into 18–20 equal-size balls, about 1 inch in diameter. The size doesn't matter too much, it's just a guideline, but make sure you press them together really firmly so that they stay together. Place them on the prepared tray as you go and then put them in the freezer for 15 minutes, or in the fridge for 30 minutes, to firm up.

+ Once they are ready, melt the chocolate in the microwave in 30-second blasts, stirring after each blast, or in a small bowl over a pan of simmering water, making sure that the bottom of the bowl does not touch the water, otherwise the chocolate may go all grainy and hard.

>

Shameless shortcut cookies-and-cream lollipops

(continued)

+ Remove the balls from the fridge/freezer. Dip the end of a lollipop stick into the melted chocolate and then push that end into a ball so it goes in about ¾ inches. Repeat with the rest of the balls, laying them back on the tray as you go.

+ Dip the balls into the remaining chocolate one at a time, swirling them about a bit and then letting the excess drip back into the bowl. Stand them up on the tray (with the sticks pointing upright).

+ If using a coating like the hundreds and thousands or chopped nuts, then have it ready in a small bowl before you coat the balls in chocolate. Once the balls are covered in the chocolate, dip them straight into the coating of choice until completely or even just half covered, whatever you fancy.

+ Return them to the freezer for 10 minutes (or the fridge for about 20 minutes) until set. If they are going into the freezer, they may need to be lying down, which is completely fine.

+ To serve, either stand them on a platter or cake stand (as they are on the tray) or put them upright in a glass so the balls are on top.

Time from start to finish:
15 minutes
Makes: 2 cups plus 2 tablespoons
Equipment: Medium saucepan,
large bowl, sieve

2 cups plus 2 tbsp whole milk

1 vanilla bean (or a few drops of
vanilla extract)

6 medium egg yolks

⅓ cup sugar

Homemade vanilla custard (crème anglaise)

This custard recipe is also great for making ice cream, so if you have an ice cream maker, you can churn it to make beautifully silky vanilla ice cream.

+ Pour the milk into a medium saucepan on a low to medium heat. Halve the vanilla bean, scrape the seeds out and add them also (you can chuck the pod in too, unless you prefer to add it to your sugar jar to make vanilla sugar) or add the vanilla extract. Leave to come slowly to the boil.

+ Meanwhile, put the egg yolks and sugar into a large bowl and mix them together gently.

+ As soon as the milk is boiling, remove it from the heat and carefully fish the vanilla bean out (if it was used). Keep the saucepan close by as you will need it again.

+ Sit the egg mixture bowl on a tea towel to stop it from spinning around and then, stirring all the time, slowly pour the milk into the egg mixture. Continue to mix it together for about 20 seconds and then pour everything back into the milk saucepan.

+ Return the pan to a very low heat and cook the custard very gently for 7–8 minutes, stirring all the time with a wooden spoon. It's important to stay with it as it could turn to scrambled eggs easily.

+ To test when it is ready, lift the wooden spoon out of the mixture. The custard should coat the back of the spoon nicely. It won't be really thick like our store-bought friend, but it will be a little thicker than heavy cream. If you want to make it thicker, put some cornstarch into a mug, add a little of the custard and then tip the whole lot back into the saucepan. Cook for a minute or so and then pour through a sieve (to get rid of any lumps). Pour the finished custard into a serving pitcher and serve hot.

Mango chutney

Time from start to finish:
20 minutes, plus a further
10 minutes if preparing your
own mangoes
Makes: 1 quart
Equipment: Large saucepan,
zester, blender or food processor,
Ball or jam jars (and their lids)
with a total capacity of 1 quart

Three 9-oz packages of prepared
mango cubes or 5 medium–large ripe
mangoes

⅔ cup sherry or apple cider vinegar

1⅓ cups granulated sugar

2 cloves

2 star anise

1 cinnamon stick

1 bunch of green onions

2 garlic cloves

3 red chillies

¾-inch piece of fresh ginger

1 orange

Salt and freshly ground black pepper

To prepare containers for the chutney, sterilize the Ball or jam jars (and their lids). I like to do this in the dishwasher on the hottest setting, or you could carefully put them in just-boiled water (off the heat) for a couple of minutes and dry with a clean towel.

+ If using whole mangoes, prepare them first (if using prepared fruit, then skip happily on to the next step). Slice the two cheeks off either side of the pit. Cut them in half and then run the knife through the flesh close to the skin to peel it. Dice the flesh into bite-size pieces and scatter on a big serving platter. I like to slice off the remaining skinny sides of mango and use them too, so as not to waste any.

+ For the chutney, pour the sherry or vinegar and sugar into a large saucepan and add the cloves, star anise and cinnamon stick. Bring slowly to the boil, stirring until the sugar dissolves.

+ Meanwhile, trim and finely slice the green onions (the green and white bits) and peel and finely chop the garlic and set aside.

+ Once boiling, turn the heat up under the saucepan and leave the vinegar mixture to boil hard for 3 minutes until thickened and syrupy.

+ Meanwhile, seed and finely chop the red chillies, peel and finely chop the ginger and finely grate the zest of the orange.

+ Stir the green onions, garlic, chillies, ginger and orange zest into the syrup along with the mango pieces. Cook at a rolling boil for 8 minutes.

+ Once the mango is soft, remove from the heat and leave to cool for a moment. Then ladle about half of the mixture into a blender or processor and pulse a few times to give a fairly smooth pulp. Stir this back into the rest of the mixture and season with salt and pepper to taste. Then ladle it into the sterilized jars.

+ Leave to cool completely in a cool place with a sheet of paper towel over the top of each jar so that the chutney can breathe but no dust or anything can get in it. Then, once cool, pop the lids on and store in a cool dry place for a couple of weeks or in the fridge for up to 1 month. You now have some really tasty mango and orange chutney!

¾ cup plus 2 tbsp butter

1¾ cups plus 2 tbsp soft light brown sugar

3 tbsp golden syrup or light corn syrup

⅔ cup light cream

½–1 tsp sea salt, to taste

Salted caramel toffee sauce

This sauce will keep in the fridge for up to a week. It will thicken on cooling, but can be rewarmed easily, so it's handy for those indulgent occasions.

+ Place the butter, sugar and syrup in a medium saucepan on a medium heat and leave to melt for a few minutes, stirring occasionally until the sugar dissolves.

+ Stir in the cream and allow to warm through for a minute or so. Then add enough of the salt to taste. There should be a good sweet and salty contrast.

+ This is delicious served warm with the Dulce & Banana Cake (see page 241) or simply with ice cream.

Time from start to finish:
40 minutes
Makes: 1¾ pounds
Equipment: Large saucepan
with lid, zester

2¾ lbs Bramley or other tart apples

⅔ cup soft light brown or granulated sugar

1 tsp ground cinnamon

1 tsp ground ginger

3 tbsp water

1 lemon

Big pat of butter

Zesty applesauce with cinnamon & ginger

This applesauce is a great filling for the "chaussons aux pommes" on page 216. I like to make a huge batch, use what I need and then freeze the rest in small portions. Great as an accompaniment to things like roast pork or cold meats.

+ Peel and quarter the apples and remove their cores. Then roughly chop them into bite-size pieces. Put them in a large saucepan with the sugar, cinnamon, ginger and 3 tablespoons of water. Stir together well, cover with the lid and put on a low to medium heat. Leave to cook for about 8 minutes.

+ After 8 minutes, remove the lid, stir well again so nothing sticks to the bottom and leave to cook for another 8 minutes or so, or until the apples are soft but not too mushy.

+ Remove the applesauce from the heat. Finely grate the zest from the lemon over to taste, stir in the butter (this balances out the acidity in the apples nicely) and leave to cool completely.

Homemade vanilla extract

Prep time: **15 minutes, plus at least 24 hours to infuse**
Makes: **About 6 ounces**
Equipment: **1-cup Ball or jam jar (with lid), small saucepan**

¼ cup dark or white rum

½ cup sugar

½ cup water

4 vanilla beans

Buying vanilla beans is not the most pleasant experience, as they do not come cheap. However, slam "vanilla beans" into any search engine and places will come up that sell them wholesale. Most people don't want to buy a whole wad of these beans, but they do sell them in "domestic" quantities. What friends of mine have done is to group together and place an order at the same time.

Once you have scraped the seeds from the bean to use in another recipe, pop the empty bean into your jar of sugar syrup. If you are an avid baker, before too long you will have lots of beans in your jar with the residual seeds left in them, making the most delicious vanilla extract you can imagine. If, however, you are impatient and keen to get going, then just follow the recipe below, buying four vanilla beans and sticking them in a jar so you can use your vanilla extract straightaway. Great to decant into little bottles (again, you can find them online), then just cut the vanilla beans in half, and give them away as presents as part of a gift basket.

+ Sterilize a Ball or jam jar (and its lid) in the dishwasher on the hottest setting or carefully put them in just-boiled water (off the heat) for a couple of minutes and dry with a clean towel.

+ Put the rum and sugar in a small saucepan with ½ cup of water. Set on a low to medium heat and stir from time to time until the sugar has dissolved. Then turn up the heat and bring to the boil. Once boiling, leave the syrup to bubble away for 5 minutes and then take it off the heat to cool a little.

+ Pour the cooled sugar syrup into the sterilized jar. Split the vanilla beans all the way down their length, add them to the syrup and leave to cool completely. Then put the lid on and leave for at least 24 hours to infuse.

Acknowledgments

Acknowledgments are always such a hard thing to write. There is a constant fear that I am going to leave out someone who has been instrumental in getting me to where I am today. So I will start by saying if I do indeed forget anyone, then please do forgive me. It has been a busy year, to say the least, with all sorts of highs and lows but through it all there has been a group of people who have kept me going through the thick of it.

First, I would like to say the most sincerest of thank-yous to the incredible team at James Grant: Nicola Ibison, Mary Bekhait, Neil Rodford, Darren Worsley, Paul Worsley, Sunil Singhvi, Riz Mansor, and Charlotte Hanbury, who came to my rescue at a time when I was lying in a proverbial heap on the floor and carried me to safety. The way the whole team has been there for me goes far beyond the reaches of just being managers and for that I will always, always be forever grateful.

Lisa Edwards, Alison Kirkham, Janice Hadlow, Rebecca Ford, Emma Swain and Nick Patten, who have been absolute rocks for me at the BBC. Thank you for believing in me and giving me this incredible platform to do what I so, so love to do: talk about food.

Pete Lawrence, Amy Joyce, Ceri Turnbull, Martin Morrison (edit producer/setting up inserts), Sophie Wells (assistant producer), Claire Martin (assistant producer), Angela Hall (production manager), Gina Waggott, Simon Weekes, Sam Key, Jamie Dobbs, Bill Rudolph, Paul Allen, Ben Sanderson, Neusa Love, Rupert Trotski (editor) and Gary Thomas, Rudi Thackeray and Helen Mooney, the set design team. And the brilliant director, Ben Warwick.

The very brilliant and superfast Michaela Bowles and her efficient and ever-smiling team: Phil Wells and Katy Ross (who were both most days), Stella Murphy, Chrissie Chung and Sammy Jo Squire.

The very precise and efficient Sharon Hearne-Smith for checking my recipes so very thoroughly.

And of course the stellar book team at HarperCollins: Victoria Barnsley, Belinda Budge, Barnaby Dawe and Carole Tonkinson, who is at the helm of my team. Thank you, Carole, for your razor-sharp instinct, your attention to detail and your constant support. Additionally Georgina Atsiaris, Martin Topping, Katrina O'Neill and Monica Green back at Hammersmith HQ. Thanks also to Katie Giovanni and Julia Azzarello for the food styling of the book and Lisa Harrison for the props. Thanks also to Diana Colbert.

Myles New . . . your photos are ace . . .

Carlos Ferraz, the pics in the book are divine—thank you for de-worzel-gummidging my hair and making it look lovely.

My love will always go out to the team at Storm Management.

Thanks also to Simon Fuller and the XIX team.

Huge hugs and love go out to all the members of my family who have been there since those early days of me arriving to the fold with a penchant for three Shredded Wheat (with no milk). Mum, Dad, Jace, Kate, Fran, Rachel, Auntie Angela, Victoria, James and my inspiring daughter Ella. And, of course, my awesome partner and my best friend, Ged.

Rodney, Tony Walker, Velm, Benjamin Christopherson, Judy Joo, Lia Peralta, Ewan Venters, Maggie Draycot, Norie Lagmay, Keith Stoll, Satya and all my friends who have been there for me . . . at all hours.

Jonathan Lomax and the team at Lomax, thank you for keeping me trim.

Thanks to all my Facebook and Twitter followers!

Big shout-out to TACT Care, Rays of Sunshine, The Prince's Trust, Barnado's and Sutton Community Farm. I hope I can help you more.

Thank you!

Lorraine

Dripping water hollows out a stone not through force but by persistence.
Ovid

Index

five-spice roasted duck breasts with cherry & Shiraz sauce 119

French onion & sage soup with croutons 65

fritters: Aussie sweet corn breakfast fritters 45

G

garlic
    bread, warm 63
    potato wedges 124

gazpacho: red pepper, tomato & basil gazpacho 60

ginger
    butternut squash 167
    ginger whipped cream 222
    lemon dressing 153
    mascarpone cream 233
    sesame & ginger noodles 193
    zesty applesauce with cinnamon & ginger 295

gingerbread pancakes with Parma ham & maple syrup 51

gnocchi: pan-fried mascarpone gnocchi with dreamy basil pesto 212

goat cheese
    goat cheese, figs & mint with balsamic drizzle 12
    goat cheese, toasted hazelnut & honey quesadillas 198
    on pizza 42

good old-fashioned burger with arugula, red onions & garlicky potato wedges 124

granola: maple, pecan & cranberry granola 280

Greek spinach, feta & pine nut pie with dill & crunchy phyllo 205

guacamole 23

H

harissa
    chicken cacciatore with harissa, bacon & rosemary 113
    hummus 20
    on pizza 42

hazelnut, vanilla & brown sugar shortbread 276

herby dumplings 127

homemade vanilla custard (crème anglaise) 292

homemade vanilla extract 296

honey
    goat cheese, toasted hazelnut & honey quesadillas 198
    honey & mustard dip 15
    honey soy-glazed salmon with sesame & ginger noodles 193

horseradish crème fraîche 84

hot-and-sour jumbo shrimp soup 59

hot-smoked trout kedgeree with green onions & basil 180

hummus
    harissa 20
    hummus with cumin & paprika 24
    on pizza 42

J

jam
    little jammy tarts 272
    sweet chilli 45

Jell-O shots
    lemoncello 27
    watermelon 28

K

kale & basil pesto 190

kedgeree: hot-smoked trout kedgeree with green onions & basil 180

L

lamb
    Lozza's lamb biryani 142
    maple and balsamic-glazed lamb chops with mint 139
    mighty moussaka 136
    rosemary roast cottage pie with a crispy rosti topping 130
    slow-roast, fast-prep leg of lamb with Aussie Chardonnay, rosemary, sage & bay 145

lasagne: butternut & sweet potato lasagne 201

leek: potato & leek vichyssoise with crispy bacon & chives 55

lemon
    lemon & ginger dressing 153
    lemon & lime poppy seed drizzle cake 247
    lemoncello Jell-O shots 27
    lovely limoncello 35

lemoncello Jell-O shots 27

lentils: warm salmon & lentils 184

let them eat cake, cake 248

lime
    coriander crème fraîche 207
    lemon & lime poppy seed drizzle cake 247

little jammy tarts 272

little warm Bramley apple pies or "chaussons aux pommes" 216

lollipops
    shameless shortcut cookies-and-cream lollipops 288
    white chocolate lollipops with dried cranberries 287

lovely limoncello 35

Lozza's lamb biryani 142

M

mackerel salad with horseradish crème fraîche 84

mango
    chutney 293
    mango, feta & avocado salad 70
    salsa 107
    Union cobb 88

maple syrup
    gingerbread pancakes with Parma ham & maple syrup 51
    maple, pecan & cranberry granola 280
    maple syrup and balsamic-glazed lamb chops with mint, toasted almonds and feta couscous 139

mascarpone
    broccoli & blue cheese soup with chive mascarpone 63
    pan-fried mascarpone gnocchi 212
    pear, almond & amaretto tart with ginger mascarpone cream 233

meringues 225
    neat-and-tidy Eton mess with blackberries 222

mighty moussaka 136

mojitos, strawberry & mint 32

Moroccan pesto fish with caramelized onions & haricot beans served with minty pine nut couscous 169

mousse: chocolate with raspberries 227

muffins, blueberry & oat 279

mushroom
    & mustard sauce, creamy 150
    vegetarian mushroom & port "faux gras" with tarragon & chestnuts 38

mustard
    Gruyère & mustard croutons 65
    honey mustard dip 15
    & mushroom sauce, creamy 150

N

naughty, naughty nachos 23

neat-and-tidy Eton mess with blackberries & ginger whipped cream 222

net bread (roti jala) 265

nifty Niçoise salad with hot-smoked trout & sundried tomatoes 87

noodles
    red pepper 179
    sesame 119
    sesame & ginger 193

O

oats
    blueberry & oat muffins 279
    maple, pecan & cranberry granola 280

olives: Aussie olive damper bread 256

onion
    caramelized, with beans 169